# INDIA A to Z

## An Alphabetical Tour of Incredible India

### Updated Edition

Text: Veena Seshadri and Vidya Mani
Illustrations: Sony Bhaskaran
Cartoons: Greystroke

PUFFIN BOOKS

An imprint of Penguin Random House

PUFFIN BOOKS

USA | Canada | UK | Ireland | Australia
New Zealand | India | South Africa | China

Puffin Books is part of the Penguin Random House group of companies
whose addresses can be found at global.penguinrandomhouse.com

Published by Penguin Random House India Pvt. Ltd
4th Floor, Capital Tower 1, MG Road,
Gurugram 122 002, Haryana, India

Penguin
Random House
India

First published in Puffin by Penguin Random House India 2013
This rejacketed edition published in Puffin by Penguin Random House India 2021

Copyright © Penguin Random House India 2013

Content researched and developed by Melting Pot, Bangalore
Text by Veena Seshadri and Vidya Mani
Illustrations by Sony Bhaskaran
Cartoons by Greystroke
Page 161 is an extension of the copyright page.

The views and opinions expressed in this book are the authors' own and the facts are as reported by them,
which have been verified to the extent possible, and the publishers are not in any way liable for the same.

ISBN 9780143332572

Typeset in Arial by Melting Pot
Printed at Tara Art Printers Pvt. Ltd. Noida-201301, India

www.penguin.co.in

# Contents

| | | | |
|---|---|---|---|
| Metros<br>Monsoon<br>Monuments<br>Musical Instruments<br>Mythical Monsters | **M**<br>**81** | **T**<br>**133** | Taj Mahal<br>Temples<br>Toys<br>Trees |
| Namaste<br>National Parks<br>National Symbols<br>Newspapers<br>Nobel Laureates | **N**<br>**91** | **U**<br>**140** | Unani Medicine<br>Union Territories<br>Universities |
| Observatories<br>Olive Ridley Turtles<br>Om | **O**<br>**100** | **V**<br>**145** | Varanasi<br>Villages |
| Paintings<br>Palaces<br>Panchatantra<br>Ports<br>Post | **P**<br>**105** | **W**<br>**148** | Wagah<br>Wazwan<br>Weddings |
| Queens<br>Qutub Minar | **Q**<br>**114** | **X**<br>**152** | X Avatars of Vishnu<br>Xuanzang |
| Railways<br>Rajasaurus<br>Rangoli<br>Religion<br>Rupee | **R**<br>**117** | **Y**<br>**156** | Yatra<br>Yoga |
| Saints<br>Sari<br>Seven Sisters<br>Spice<br>Sundarbans | **S**<br>**125** | **Z**<br>**159** | Zero<br>Zoos |

# AUTHORS' NOTE

Bharat. Hindustan. Jambudweep. Down the ages, India has been known by all these names . . . besides being called the Land of Spices, the Land of Festivals and the Land of Seven Rivers. This vast, vibrant country, rich in marvels both natural and man-made, has a culture that goes back more than 5000 years. It has also been ruled by some of the mightiest dynasties. So it comes as no surprise that we encounter innumerable wonders, mysteries and puzzles throughout India!

This book is a celebration of the country's treasures, both ancient and modern. As you can imagine, we could not possibly squeeze in *all* of them into a single book. Then why have we chosen to call it *India: A to Z*?

Good question! Now, close your eyes and imagine you are at your favourite food court. Someone orders all the goodies available there, and tells you that you can have a bite of every single thing there is to eat. Wouldn't that be cool? Well, we are aiming to do something similar in our book. We are going to give you little titbits of information about all the important things that capture the essence of India. And we hope it will get you started on a lifelong journey of discovery.

From the Aadhar card to the oldest zoo, from Bollywood to yoga, from Indian dinosaurs to our mythical monsters, the book has interesting information, funky facts and trivia treats from every region in the country. They will give you an exciting overview of India and its history, fairs and festivals, monuments and myths, art and architecture, wildlife and wonders, its movers and shakers and much more. Get ready to sample everything from the awesome to the zany, from the fabulous to the funny, from the groovy to the gory, and from the saintly to the scary. What's more, there are cool cartoons and beautiful photographs that lend colour to the pages of this fun-tastic book! Curious kya? Then, flip the page, and have a blast on your alphabetical tour of Incredible India!

**Veena Seshadri**                    **Vidya Mani**

# A
## for Aadhaar

What makes you uniquely Indian? The fact that you are reading *India: A to Z*? Good reason that, but there's an even better one—your 12-digit individual identification number called Aadhaar!

## WHAT'S IN A NUMBER?

Everything if you're Indian and have an Aadhar number! That's right, your 12-digit individual identification number issued by the Unique Identification Authority of India (UIDAI) serves as a proof of your identity and address, anywhere in India. Each Aadhaar number is unique to an individual and will remain valid for life.

Why did the UIDAI (a part of the Planning Commission of India) come up with this idea? Well, since we have so many different proofs of identity, they felt that every permanent Indian resident should have a single source of identity verification. And so, in February 2009, they launched a project to issue a unique number linked to a resident's demographic and biometric information. The number can be used as proof of identity and will provide access to a host of benefits and services in banking, telecommunication, processing of passport applications, etc. Nandan Nilekani, former co-chairman of Infosys Technologies, was appointed the first chairman of the UIDAI in June 2009.

YES, I'M CALLING FROM THE DELHI OFFICE. HAVE YOU SPOKEN TO 348961374990 ABOUT 89073456789? I HAD SENT THE FILE TO 356122783459 THREE DAYS BACK ...

## NUMBER CRUNCHER

The Aadhaar number project is the largest personal identification programme the world has ever witnessed. Over 1.3 billion people are eligible to receive an Aadhar card. The Indian government will spend approximately Rs 113 per person who enrols to get an Aadhar card. That adds up to about Rs 1,46,90,00,00,000 (14,690 crore rupees) if all of India's 1.3 billion residents sign up for the card!

**AADHAAR**

## AH, AADHAAR!

• The UIDAI launched the Aadhaar scheme in the small tribal village of Tembhli in Maharashtra. The first Indian to receive the card was Ranjana Sonawane, a resident of this village.

• The total number of Aadhaar cards issued as of 2019 is nearly 123 crore. That means, almost 95 per cent of India's population has one!

• Aadhaar's logo is a sun in red and yellow, with a fingerprint traced across its centre. The logo represents a new dawn of equal opportunity for each individual in India.

# A for Adivasi

**Little is known of their history, but what we do know for a fact is that the Adivasi people were among the original inhabitants of the Indian subcontinent.**

## FIRST THINGS FIRST

Adivasi is the collective name used for the many indigenous peoples of India. The term 'Adivasi' comes from the Hindi word 'adi' which means from the beginning and 'vasi' which means inhabitant. The word was coined in the 1930s to create a sense of identity among the various native peoples of India.

If they were among the first residents of our country, why were they pushed to the outer edges of society? According to historians, it appears that their land was encroached upon by Indo-Aryan tribes some 3000 years ago. The Adivasi people were driven away into the mountains and hill areas after these invasions. As a result they underwent major changes in their traditional ways of life and became vulnerable to economic exploitation.

In 1950, the Constitution of India identified most of these groups as people who required social and economic development. Since that time, the Adivasi people have been officially known as Scheduled Tribes and have been given many protective provisions. In the Lok Sabha and the Rajya Sabha, 7 per cent of the total number of seats are reserved for members of the scheduled tribes.

EKALAVYA TAUGHT ME THIS: *WHERE THERE IS A BHIL, THERE IS A WAY!*

## ARE THEY ONE PEOPLE?

The Adivasi people are not a homogeneous group. There are believed to be over 200 distinct peoples speaking more than 100 languages. According to a recent census, the Adivasi people constitute 8 per cent of India's population, which means there are over 84 million of them. A majority of them live in the states of Chattisgarh, Jharkhand, Madhya Pradesh, Orissa and in the North-Eastern states of Arunachal Pradesh, Nagaland and Mizoram. The largest groups of Adivasi people are the **Bhil**, the **Munda** and the **Santhal**.

*The Bhils live all over western and central India.*

## ADIVASI ACHIEVERS

• The Mahabharata mentions that **Eklavya** was a Bhil, who taught himself archery standing before the clay image of the great teacher Dronacharya. Eklavya went on to achieve a greater level of skill than Drona's favourite student, Arjuna.

• **Shabari** was a Bhil woman. She offered Rama and Lakshmana jujubes when the brothers were searching for Sita in the Dandakaranya forest, in present-day Gujarat.

• **Birsa Munda** was a tribal freedom fighter, who belonged to the Munda tribe. His portrait hangs in the Central Hall of Parliament, the only tribal leader to have been given the honour.

# for Ajanta

Cut into the sides of cliffs located in the middle of nowhere in Maharashtra are two of India's most magnificent and most visited cave temples—Ajanta and Ellora.

## BUDDHIST WONDER

The **Ajanta Caves** are regarded among the most impressive Buddhist monuments in India. These 30 rock-cut caves demonstrate the skill and artistry that Indian craftsmen had achieved hundreds of years ago, especially since it is believed that they used nothing more than a chisel and a hammer to carve them! The caves were built in two phases between the 2nd century BCE and 6th century CE as chaityas (chapels for praying) and viharas (monasteries for living and teaching) for Buddhist monks.

The Ajanta Caves were excavated on a horseshoe-shaped rock surface and rise up to a height of 250 feet, overlooking River Waghora. All the caves were originally connected to the river through ladders or flights of stairs!

## RELIGIOUS MEDLEY

A series of 34 magnificent rock-cut temples located some 80 km south-west of the Ajanta Caves, the **Ellora Caves** are an uninterrupted series of monuments dug side by side in the wall of a high basalt cliff. There are 12 Buddhist caves (in the south), 17 Hindu temples (in the centre) and five Jain temples (in the north), all of which were built by the Rashtrakutas between 600 and 1000 CE.

The most spectacular of them all, the Kailasanatha Temple, was a project begun by King Krishna I around 760 CE. The two-storey structure is carved from a single rock and is said to have taken a hundred years to complete!

An exquisite sculpture of Shiva and Parvati at Ellora

A beautiful fresco in one of the Ajanta Caves

## WHAT MAKES AJANTA ASTONISHING

Even more beautiful than the architecture are the paintings in the caves, which depict stories from the Jataka Tales and events from the life of the Buddha. Even though they were done some 2000 years ago, the colours still retain a shine!

## WHAT MAKES ELLORA ENCHANTING

Not only is Ellora a marvel of art and technology, it is also a testimony to ancient India's spirit of religious tolerance. The complex contains temples devoted to three religions (Buddhism, Hinduism and Jainism) all within a single site!

# A

## for Armed Forces

**They safeguard our country's borders by patrolling them on land, air and water. They defend our country from foreign attack. They help rescue people in time of disasters. Who are these brave men and women who risk their lives every day for the country? India's amazing armed forces, of course.**

## ARMED AND AVAILABLE

The Indian armed forces are the military forces of the country. They consist of the **Army**, **Navy** and **Air Force**. Paramilitary forces like the Indian Coast Guard, Assam Rifles and Special Frontier Force and some inter-service units are part of the armed forces too. The President of India is the supreme commander of the country's armed forces. But the forces are primarily managed by the Ministry of Defence, and headed by their respective chiefs of staff.

## CORE COMMANDS

The Indian armed forces are split into different groups based on where they operate. The Indian Army is divided into seven commands, each under the control of different lieutenant generals, for the purpose of administration. The Indian Air Force is split into five operational and two functional commands, each headed by an air officer commanding-in-chief of the rank of air marshal. The Indian Navy operates three commands, which are headed by a flag officer commanding-in-chief of the rank of vice admiral. There are two joint commands whose head can belong to any of the three services. These are the Strategic Forces Command and the Andaman and Nicobar Command.

## ARMED FORCES IN ACTION

The armed forces have five main tasks: to safeguard the territorial integrity of India, to defend the country if it is attacked by external or internal enemies, to quickly mobilize forces and take action without crossing the enemy's nuclear threshold, to assist civil society in case of disasters, and to participate in UN peacekeeping operations.

A regiment of the Indian Army marching in military precision during a parade

## INCREDIBLE INFO

• The Indian armed forces are currently the world's largest arms importer. Russia, Israel, France and the US are the primary suppliers of our military equipment.

• India honours its armed forces and military personnel annually on Armed Forces Flag Day on 7 December.

• The Indian Army is the third biggest military contingent in the world after USA and China.

• Sachin Tendulkar was the first civilian without an aviation background to be awarded the honorary rank of group captain by the Indian Air Force.

• The 17th century Maratha warrior-king Chhatrapati Shivaji is considered the Father of the Indian Navy.

# for Aryabhata

**A pioneering mathematician and astronomer, Aryabhata was the man who gave the world the concept of zero. He also came up with the laws of planetary motion in the 5th century CE—a good 1000 years before Johannes Kepler and Galileo Galilei announced the same thing!**

## WRITTEN IN THE STARS?

Do you think Aryabhata was destined to become India's most acclaimed mathematician and astronomer? He was born in a small place called Taregana in Bihar, although some historians think he was born in South India. Would you believe that 'Taregana' actually translates to song of the stars in Hindi? Little wonder then that Aryabhata reached for the stars when it came to the study of mathematics and astronomy! His most famous contributions include the theory that the earth rotates on its axis, explanations of the solar and lunar eclipses, solving of quadratic equations, place-value system with zero, and the value of pi.

India's first satellite, Aryabhata, was launched in April 1975.

## POETRY IN NUMBERS

Although nothing much is known about his personal life, it is fairly certain that Aryabhata lived and worked at Kusumapura near Pataliputra during the Golden Age of the Guptas. And that's where he wrote his two most well-known works, the *Aryabhatiya* and the now lost *Aryabhatasiddhanta*.

The *Aryabhatiya* is a small treatise composed of 118 verses, which describes in detail the mathematics of the time. It begins with a 10-verse introduction, followed by a mathematical section written in 33 verses that explains 66 mathematical rules of algebra, arithmetic, plane trigonometry, spherical trigonometry, continued fractions, quadratic equations and more. The next section consists of 25 verses which elucidate the planetary models. The final section of the book contains 50 verses in which he interprets lunar and solar eclipses accurately. And all this in poetry!

## ZERO HERO

Aryabhata's greatest contribution was the concept of zero, which he came up with around 500 CE. He did not use the symbol we use today, but mathematicians agree that his idea of zero was clearly based on how he developed his place-value system. Good for us, because you can imagine how much more annoying maths would be if we had to calculate everything using Roman numerals!

# for Aryabhata

## HURRAH TO ARYABHATA

India's first satellite, which was launched in 1975, is named after Aryabhata. So is a crater on the moon. A well-known institute for conducting research in astronomy, astrophysics and atmospheric sciences is the Aryabhatta Research Institute of Observational Sciences near Nainital. What's more, a species of bacteria discovered by ISRO scientists in 2009 has also been named *Bacillus aryabhata* after him!

## THE FIRST INDIAN IN SPACE

Centuries later, in April 1984, a young Indian stepped into a Soviet spaceship, blasted off into space and entered our history books! As part of a historic joint space programme between the Indian Space Research Organization and Soviet Intercosmos, Squadron Leader **Rakesh Sharma** was selected to become the first Indian to go into space. Launched along with two Soviet cosmonauts aboard *Soyuz T-11*, Sharma spent seven days, 21 hours and 40 minutes in space on the *Salyut* 7 space station and conducted an earth observation programme focusing on India.

Besides tough physical training sessions and detailed space lessons, the instruction process to be part of this mission included a three-month language learning programme in the course of which Sharma had to speak Russian eight hours a day!

During his stay in space, when Prime Minister Indira Gandhi asked him how India looked from up there, Sharma said, 'Saare Jahan se Achcha', making every Indian proud.

*Rakesh Sharma, India's first astronaut*

## DESTINATION MOON

On 22 October 2008, India became one of the few countries to put a satellite in orbit around the moon. *Chandrayaan-1* was our first unmanned lunar probe. Launched by the Indian Space Research Organization from the Satish Dhawan Space Centre, in Sriharikota, *Chandrayaan-1* announced to the world that India had researched and developed its own technology to explore the moon. On 8 November 2008, the mission's most difficult part went off smoothly and the probe started orbiting around the earth's only natural satellite. With that, India became the fourth country to place its flag on the moon.

*Chandrayaan-1* operated for 312 days as opposed to the intended two years, but it achieved many of its objectives, the most significant of which was the discovery of water molecules in lunar soil. Encouraged by its success, ISRO went on to successfully develop and launch *Mangalyaan*, a space probe orbiting Mars, in 2013, and are currently working on *Gaganyaan*, India's first manned spacecraft.

## for Bazaars

**Hundreds of products big and small, thousands of sellers vying to grab your attention, lakhs of buyers haggling at all decibel levels . . . Welcome to the great Indian bazaar, a colourful and crowded cultural phenomenon like no other!**

## BANGLES BECKON

Set in one of the by-lanes that surround the historic Charminar in Hyderabad, the **Laad Bazaar** or Choodi Bazaar is one of India's oldest marketplaces. The bazaar, which is over 400 years old, is believed to have been set up by a former ruler, Mohammed Quli Qutub Shah, as a shopping destination for guests who had been invited to attend his daughter's wedding! The doting dad named the bazaar after his darling daughter Laad.

Laad, which also means lacquer, is what is used to make most of the beautiful bangles sold here, on which glittering artificial gems are studded. These handcrafted lac bangles are made by experienced craftsmen whose families have been fashioning them for generations. A recent addition to the bangle list are the popular lightweight bangles made of artificial gold and silver. Sellers claim that a single sneeze can send these bangles flying six feet high in the air while a hearty laugh can blow them eight feet away!

*The iconic Charminar overlooks Laad Bazaar.*

## TREASURES FROM THIEVES

Looking for rare antiques, vintage coins, Bollywood posters and an endless array of trinkets and treasures? Step into the crammed lanes of Mumbai's famous **Chor Bazaar**, which literally translates as Thieves' Market. Make sure you have enough time on your hands though, because most shopkeepers here are in no hurry to sell their wares. They would much rather chat for hours about the history of the bazaar. Many say the place used to be called Shor Bazaar (noisy market), but became Chor Bazaar because the British could not pronounce the name correctly!

Eventually, however, stolen goods started finding their way into the market, making it live up to its new name. A popular story goes that a violin belonging to Queen Victoria went missing while being unloaded from the ship when she was on a visit to Bombay. It later turned up for sale at Chor Bazaar!

MISTER, YOU ASK ME ONE MORE TIME AND I'LL HAVE *VIOLENCE* FOR YOU, NOT *VIOLINS!*

## for Bazaars

# MARKET BY MOONLIGHT

**Chandni Chowk**, which means moonlit square or market, is one of the oldest and busiest markets in Old Delhi. Built in the 17th century by the great Mughal Emperor Shah Jahan and designed by his daughter Jahan Ara, the market was once divided by canals (now closed) which reflected the moonlight. It remains one of India's largest wholesale market famous for zari saris, books, leather goods, electronic items, and most important of all, sweets and confectionary for all tastes!

An interesting mansion located inside the market is the Khazanchi Haveli. The khazanchis who lived there were Shah Jahan's accountants. A long underground tunnel connects their haveli and the Red Fort, so that money could be transferred safely! Equally interesting is the fact that a mosque (Jama Masjid), a Jain temple (Sri Digambar Jain Lal Mandir), a church (Christian Central Baptist Church), a Hindu temple (Gauri Shankar Temple) and a gurudwara (Gurudwara Sis Ganj Sahib) all coexist quite peacefully within the market premises.

*Snacks and sweets aplenty at Delhi's bustling Chandni Chowk*

# BAZAAR BUZZ

• Famed for its diamond polishing and cutting industry, Surat is often called the Antwerp of the East. At the bustling **Mahidharpura Diamond Market**, diamonds (from big stones to small fragments to powder) worth millions of rupees are traded right on the streets!

• The **Khwairamband Bazaar** in Imphal is Manipur's main market. A unique feature of this market is that all the stalls are owned and run by women.

• The **Wednesday Flea Market** at Anjuna Beach has an interesting story behind its origin. Anjuna became a hippie hotspot in the 1960s. Finding their wallets empty but wishing to enjoy the sun and sand of Goa for a little longer, the hippies started selling their clothes, jewellery, guitars and more to earn money, thus setting up the flea market!

• The best way to get to **Jain Street** in Kannauj (a small town on the banks of River Ganga) is to let your nose lead you to it! Lined with ancient perfume houses selling fragrant attar, the market has made Kannauj the perfume capital of India.

• Chennai's **Burma Bazaar** is the best place to pick up the latest gadgets and gizmos, the prices of which are determined by your bargaining skills! This market dates back to the 1960s when the government set up shops to rehabilitate Tamil refugees from Burma.

# for Beaches

Bounded by the Indian Ocean, Arabian Sea and the Bay of Bengal, India has one of the world's longest coastlines, measuring 7517 km! So what does that mean? That beaches in our country are countless in number and there's a different one to go to every time you want to have fun in the sun!

## GOA GALA

Goa might be India's tiniest state, but the one thing it is big on is beaches! There's one to suit every taste, so if hip and happening seasides are your cup of tea, **Baga** in north Goa with its shacks, water sport activities and night clubs is where you should be.

Picturesque **Palolem** beach, enclosed by a thick forest of coconut palms in far south Goa, is often believed to be the state's most beautiful seashore. And if sun and sand isn't enough, unspoilt **Agonda** has a freshwater lagoon too!

## ISLAND PARADISE

Located in the Bay of Bengal about 900 km from India, the Andaman and Nicobar Islands have some of India's finest beaches. **Radha Nagar** beach at Havelock Island has been described as the 'Best Beach in Asia' by *Time* magazine. What's more, if you're lucky, you could meet Rajan, India's only snorkelling elephant, here. Rajan cleverly uses his trunk as a snorkel to swim under water and see Havelock's colourful marine creatures!

Approximately 450 km off the western coast of Kerala, Lakshadweep is made up of 36 beautiful coral islands that shimmer like emeralds in the blue Laccadive Sea. The picture-perfect white beaches in **Agatti**, one of Lakshadweep's most beautiful lagoons, are just where you should scuba-dive or snorkel to see the amazing coral formations. Then, sit back and simply chill!

## TEMPLE TOWN BEACHES

**Mahabalipuram**, which lies to the south of Chennai in Tamil Nadu, has the best of the beaches on the east coast. The town is full of exquisite rock-cut temples, including the splendid Shore Temple, which is right on the water's edge.

At the mouth of River Malpe, about 6 km from the temple town of Udupi in Karnataka, lies an endless stretch of golden sand fringed by palm trees. **Malpe** beach has everything that a perfect seaside vacation needs—surf, sand and serenity!

Gokarna, a small holy town in the northern part of Karnataka, has some of India's most secluded beaches, including the panoramic **Om** beach, which gets its name because it is shaped like the Om symbol.

*The beach shaped like an 'Om' at Gokarna in Karnataka*

## for Beaches

INDIA IS THE LAND OF BEACHES! WHEN IT RAINS ALL OF OUR ROADS BECOME BEACHES!

*The scenic and serene Kovalam beach in Kerala*

## COASTING IN KERALA

Located 10 km off Thiruvananthapuram, the crescent-shaped sands and gentle surf of **Kovalam** beach are just what it takes to see that Kerala is not just its backwaters. **Varkala** beach, which is close by, is well known for its mineral springs and rocky cliffs, and provides a more peaceful alternative to Kovalam.

Besides being the place to catch a beautiful sunset, the beach at **Kozhikode** has great historical significance. It was here that Vasco da Gama landed, in his search for spices.

**Muzhappilangad** beach near Bekal in Kerala is said to be Asia's longest drive-in beach. It offers you the rare experience of driving on a sandy stretch parallel to the sea for a distance of about 4 km.

## BEACH BLAST

• **Chandipur** in Orissa has one of the world's most unusual beaches. Thanks to its geography, the sea can retreat up to 5 km at low tide, revealing a vast seabed filled with shells, driftwood and tiny crabs!

• The **East Coast Road**, also referred to as ECR, is a scenic highway that is built along the Bay of Bengal, and is dotted with several beaches. The total length of the highway is 690 km and it connects Chennai to Thoothukudi via Pondicherry.

• **Dona Paula** in Goa is considered to be a beach for lovers. It is named after the daughter of a viceroy, Dona Paula de Menzes, who fell in love with a local fisherman. Since she could not marry him, she committed suicide at this place, and the beach came to be regarded as a symbol of eternal love.

• With a length of 13 km, which includes a 6 km promenade, **Marina** beach in Chennai is India's longest beach and the world's second longest one.

• **Chowpatty** beach, adjoining the scenic Marine Drive, is Mumbai's oldest seafront. Famous for its chaat and kulfi stalls, the beach is also the place where thousands of Ganesha idols are immersed every year after the Ganesh Chaturthi celebrations.

# for Bhopal Gas Tragedy

**On 3 December 1984, about 45 tonnes of the dangerous gas methyl isocyanate escaped from a pesticide plant owned by Union Carbide India in Bhopal, killing approximately 20,000 people. The Bhopal gas tragedy is considered one of the worst industrial disasters in human history.**

## A DARK, DEADLY NIGHT

It was a cold night in Bhopal. A little past midnight, an operator in the Union Carbide factory's methyl isocyanate (MIC) unit noticed something going wrong. The gauge on the control panel indicated that the pressure was building up very quickly inside tank E610, which contained the lethal MIC liquid. He sounded the alarm, but by then the liquid, which had to be kept close to zero degrees centigrade, had reached a temperature of over 100 degrees! The tank was vibrating so hard that its safety reinforcement cracked. Everyone fled the factory in panic . . .

## PRICE OF NEGLIGENCE

How many people died that night? It is impossible to arrive at a conclusive figure, but eyewitnesses say that around 3000 people died at once. Approximately another 8000 passed away within the next two weeks and some 8000 people lost their lives subsequently to gas-related diseases.

In an out-of-court settlement on 14 February 1989, it was agreed that Union Carbide would pay $470 million to the Government of India. This sparked waves of protest across the country because our government's earlier claim was for $3000 million. The ultimate tragedy, however, was that the money never reached most of the victims' families.

## FIVE DEADLY SINS

At 39 degrees, liquid MIC turned into a poisonous gas and tried to escape from the tank. The factory had five safety systems in place to prevent the poisonous gas from reaching the outside air, but not one of them worked. Why?

• MIC had to be stored at a temperature of under 15 degrees. The factory had a refrigeration system that was designed to maintain this temperature. But it had been closed down as part of a cost-cutting measure.

• A spare tank was kept empty to divert any excess MIC into it. But, in the panic, nobody thought of opening the valve to allow the MIC to escape into the empty tank.

• The tank with MIC was attached by a pipe to a 30 m high chimney, where a flame was always burning. In case of a leak, the flame would burn all the gas before it reached the outside air. But the pipe was corroded and had been removed for replacement.

• The tank had a vent gas scrubber that would detoxify any leaking gas before it escaped, but it had been switched off.

• The workers tried to operate a water curtain, which would absorb the gas before it reached the air. But it only reached a height of 15 m, while the MIC gas was rushing out at a height of 33 m.

# for Bollywood

**Approximately 15 million Indians go to the movies every day! And a large number of the films they watch are made in Bollywood, India's thriving Hindi film industry in Mumbai.**

## GOLLY, OURS IS BOLLY!

The word 'Bollywood' is derived from a combination of Bombay (the former name for Mumbai) and Hollywood, the centre of the American film industry. However, unlike Hollywood, Bollywood does not exist as a physical place.

The word 'Bollywood' was first coined in the 1970s when India overtook the USA as the largest producer of films in the world! It went on to become a popular nickname for our Hindi film industry, which is based in Mumbai. The word 'Bollywood' was recently added to the Oxford English Dictionary.

BUT *SANDALWOOD** HAS ALWAYS BEEN IN THE DICTIONARY!

\* the informal name of the Kannada film industry

## BIGGER, BRIGHTER, BETTER

We often hear the fact that Bollywood is the biggest film industry in the world, producing about 1000 films a year. This isn't strictly correct. It is the Indian film industry (which includes more than 20 regional language industries) that produces these many films a year, of which Bollywood produces approximately 250. The Indian film industry sold 3.2 billion movie tickets last year, making it a bigger movie market than USA and Canada combined!

EVERY TIME I WATCH A HINDI FILM AND CRY, I FEEL THEY SHOULD CALL IT *BAWLY-WOOD* INSTEAD!

## FILMI FUNDAS

• Bollywood produced its first movie in 1899, while Hollywood's first movie was released seven years later in 1907.

• The earliest Bollywood film was made by a portrait photographer named Harischandra Sakharam Bhatavdekar. Called *The Wrestlers*, it was actually a simple and short recording of a local wrestling match.

• *Raja Harishchandra* by Dadasaheb Phalke was the first feature film made in India. It was a silent film made in 1913, which is why we're celebrating 100 years of Indian cinema in 2013. Dadasaheb Phalke found his heroine in a man called Anna Salunke at a canteen in Bombay. Salunke played the role of Queen Taramati in *Raja Harishchandra*.

• *Alam Ara*, directed by Ardeshir Irani, was India's first film with sound. It hit the screen in 1931. Six years later, Irani made *Kisan Kanya*, the first Indian film in colour.

• *LOC Kargil* is a 2003 Bollywood film based on the Kargil war. With a running time of four hours and 15 minutes, it is the longest Indian film ever made.

• The song *Ab tumhare hawale watan saathiyon* in the film by the same name is the longest Hindi film song. It is 20 minutes long and features in three instalments in the film!

# for Buddha

**Both the Buddha and Mahavira were young men born into royalty. Both renounced their kingdoms and went on to achieve enlightenment. Eventually, they became two of the world's greatest spiritual teachers.**

## FROM MONARCH TO MONK

**Prince Siddhartha** was born in 623 BCE in Lumbini in present-day Nepal. At his naming ceremony, eight wise men predicted that the infant would grow up to become a great emperor or a much-admired holy man. So his father did everything he could to keep his son away from the realities of life. Siddhartha was given new clothes to wear every day and new palaces were built for him to live in every time the seasons changed!

One day, Siddhartha saw an old man, a sick person and a corpse, and realized that the world was filled with suffering. He then came across an ascetic, who had renounced the world, so that he could be released from human misery. On learning this, Siddhartha left his palace in search of the real meaning of life. He was only 29 at the time. He travelled across India for six years, and finally, when he was meditating under a peepal tree at Bodh Gaya, he found the truth or nirvana he was looking for. In that moment of enlightenment, Siddhartha became the Buddha or he who is awake.

Hindus believe that the Buddha was an incarnation of Lord Vishnu.

## FROM ARISTOCRAT TO ASCETIC

Much like Prince Siddhartha of Lumbini, **Prince Vardhamana** too was born into royalty in 599 BCE in Kundalagrama, Bihar. He was the son of King Siddhartha and Queen Trishala of the Nata clan. He got the name Mahavira or Great Warrior in his boyhood when he tamed a serpent single-handedly. At the age of 30, he suddenly abandoned his family and all the comforts of royal life and left home in search of spiritual awakening.

It is said that as part of his rigorous penance, he wore only one garment for more than a year and later went naked. He even allowed insects to crawl over his body and bite him, bearing the pain with patience. Finally, after 12 years of extreme asceticism, he attained kevala or supreme knowledge.

A statue of the Jain spiritual teacher, Mahavira

## WHY DOES THE WORLD NEED THEM?

The 7th to 5th centuries BCE were a time of great social upheaval in India. The kshatriyas rebelled against the domination of the brahmins who claimed to be superior by virtue of their birth. In particular, there was great opposition to the large-scale Vedic sacrifices that involved the killing of animals. That is why the philosophy of ahimsa or non-violence preached by both the Buddha and Mahavira appealed greatly to the people. Don't you think this is why their teachings are relevant even today?

## for Chess

**Chaturanga, a game based on the Indian style of warfare, and whose pieces represented the infantry, cavalry, chariots and elephants, was invented in Gupta times around the 6th century CE. Today, it is called chess!**

## CARE FOR A GAME OF CHATURANGA?

Chaturanga, an ancient Indian game, is believed to be the ancestor of chess. From India, it travelled to Persia, where it was called shatranj. It subsequently reached Western Europe in the late medieval period, where it evolved into the game as we know it today. In fact, 'shah mat' in Persian literally translates to 'the king has been ambushed'. This is probably the origin of the 'checkmate' in chess!

Where did the idea of the game come from? Well, straight from the battleground! The name chaturanga comes from a battle formation mentioned in the Mahabharata, referring to four divisions of an army. The game, in its early stages, was played on an 8 × 8 uncheckered board, called the ashtapada. The exact rules of chaturanga are not known, although chess historians believe that its rules were similar to those of its successor, shatranj, on which many books were written in Persia.

Banabhatta's *Harsha Charitha*, written in 625 CE, contains the earliest reference to the name chaturanga.

WHEN YOU SAID *SHAH MAT*, I THOUGHT YOU MEANT THE KING WANTED TO SLEEP ON A MAT!

## CHATURANGA OR CHATURAJI?

Chaturaji, meaning 'four kings', is a four player chess-like game. It was first described by Al Beruni in his book, *Tarikh Al-Hind* (History of India), which detailed his travels in India. Some chess historians argue that chaturaji is a predecessor of chaturanga and hence the ancestor of modern chess. However, this theory has been rejected by most modern scholars, who believe that chaturanga was a game by itself and is indeed the root of chess.

Some forms of Chaturanga were played with dice.

## CHAMPION OF CHAMPIONS

**Viswanathan Anand** is an Indian chess Grandmaster and a former five-time classical world chess champion. Anand has won the World Chess Championship five times (in 2000, 2007, 2008, 2010 and 2012). He is also the only chess player in the history of the game who has won the World Championship in three different formats—knockout, tournament and match. Anand also became the World Rapid Chess Champion in 2003, which was the first speedy time-bound tournament conducted by FIDE (the world's chess federation).

At the Amber chess tournament which uniquely combines blindfold chess and speed chess, Viswanathan Anand is the only player to have won both the rapid and blindfold events in the same year. He did it twice, in 1997 and then in 2005!

# for Churches

How did Christianity come to India? Well, the story goes that Doubting Thomas, one of the 12 apostles of Christ, came to Kerala way back in 52 CE, established the religion and built many beautiful churches as places of worship for the Christians.

## THOMAS' TRIUMPH

So where was the first church in the country set up? The **St Thomas Syro-Malabar Catholic Church** at Palayoor in the Thrissur district of Kerala was established in 52 CE by St Thomas, who was also called Doubting Thomas. He was given this name because he did not believe that Jesus would be resurrected after his crucifixion until he saw Jesus with his own eyes again! After that, he travelled all over the world to spread the glory of Christ. The Palayoor Church that he built is believed to be India's oldest church and is even older than the Catholic Church in Rome. It is an Apostolic Church from where St Thomas preached Christ's message. Besides the church at Palayoor, St Thomas also built six other churches across Kerala and Tamil Nadu.

Built by Portuguese explorers over the tomb of St Thomas at Santhome in Chennai in the 16th century, the **San Thome Basilica** was later made into a cathedral by the British in 1893. St Thomas is believed to have been martyred here while spreading the tenets of Christianity. Redesigned by the British in a Neo-Gothic style, the church has beautiful stained glass panels depicting various stages of St Thomas' life and a statue of Virgin Mary that traces its origin to Portugal.

The St Thomas Syro-Malabar Catholic Church

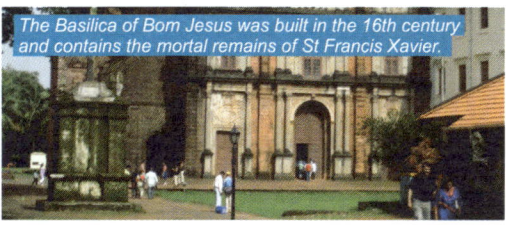
The Basilica of Bom Jesus was built in the 16th century and contains the mortal remains of St Francis Xavier.

## GOA'S GLORY

Old Goa or Velha Goa is a UNESCO World Heritage Site and has spectacular churches and convents, which are known for their exquisite architecture and historical importance. Some of the important ones include **Basilica of Bom Jesus**, **Se Cathedral**, **Church of St Francis of Assisi**, **Chapel of St Catherine** and **Church of Our Lady of Divine Providence**.

The **Basilica of Bom Jesus** is one of the most famous churches in India and is over 400 years old. Built in the 16th century and dedicated to Infant Jesus, the basilica is an impressive and elaborately carved structure. The enshrined mortal remains of St Francis Xavier, the patron saint of Goa, is one of the church's treasures. His body is placed in a well-decorated silver casket, which is kept on the right side of the altar. It attracts a huge number of devotees from all over the world.

Right opposite the Basilica of Bom Jesus is the **Se Cathedral**. The church was under construction for nearly three-fourths of a century beginning from 1562. Dedicated to St Catherine, the Se Cathedral is one of the largest churches in Asia. In the cathedral's tower is the remarkable Golden Bell, which can be heard up to Panjim (Goa's capital) 14 km away! Yet, when you stand next to the bell, its sound is just a soft tinkle!

# for Churches

An inside view of the St Francis CSI Church in Fort Kochi, where Vasco da Gama was first buried.

## MIGHTY MIRACLES

Located in the coastal town of Velankanni in Tamil Nadu, the **Basilica of Our Lady of Good Health** is one of India's most sacred churches. Called the Lourdes of the East, devotees light candles inside the church to pray to Mother Mary to cure ailments big and small. A nine-day festival that takes place at the church every year between end August and early September attracts almost two million pilgrims!

Why do so many people flock to the church? Thanks to three miracles that are believed to have taken place in and around where the basilica stands. An apparition of Mother Mary and Infant Jesus that appeared as a vision to a sleeping shepherd boy, a lame buttermilk vendor being cured by Mother Mary and Child Jesus and the rescue of a shipful of Portuguese soldiers caught in a violent storm in the Bay of Bengal! Remarkably, all these extraordinary events are said to have taken place on 8 September, the day of the feast of the birth of the Blessed Virgin Mary.

The Velankanni Basilica is called the Lourdes of the East because a large number of pilgrims visit the church, much like Lourdes Church in France.

## FASCINATING FIRSTS

• The world's oldest existing church-like structure was believed to have been built by St Thomas in 57 CE. It was named **Thiruvithamcode Arappally** or Thomaiyar Kovil by Uthiyan Cheralathan, the first Chera king. It is located at Thiruvithamcode in Kanyakumari district of Tamil Nadu and is presently an international pilgrim centre.

• The **St Francis CSI Church** in Fort Kochi, originally built in 1503, is the oldest European church in India. The Portuguese explorer, Vasco da Gama, died in Kochi in 1524, when he was on his third visit to India. His body was first buried in this church, but the remains were shifted to Lisbon 14 years later.

• The first Protestant missionaries to set foot in India were two Lutherans from Germany, **Bartholomäus Ziegenbalg** and **H**einrich Plütschau. They who came to the Danish settlement of Tranquebar in 1705 and established a mission there. Today, the Bishop of Tranquebar is the official title of the bishop of the Tamil Evangelical Lutheran Church in Tamil Nadu, which was founded in 1919 as a result of the work that the two first Lutherans did.

# for Constitution

**Do you know why we celebrate Republic Day in January? On 26 January 1950, India became a republic because that was the day our constitution came into force. The Constitution of India is the highest law in the land and tells us in detail how the country should be governed.**

## CONSTITUTION OF OUR CONSTITUTION

Is the constitution just a bunch of fuddy-duddy laws that tell us how the country should be run? Not really, India's constitution is unique and is made up of several interesting parts!

The **Preamble** is an introduction to the constitution and declares that India is a sovereign, socialist, secular, democratic republic. It sums up the goals of the government as liberty, equality and justice for everyone, and the promotion of national unity through fraternity or friendship among all.

The **Directive Principles of State Policy** aim to create a welfare state. These are guidelines to the central and state governments of India, which are to be kept in mind while framing laws and policies.

The constitution gives every Indian citizen six **Fundamental Rights**—the right to equality, the right to freedom, the right to freedom of religion, the right against exploitation, cultural and educational rights and the right to constitutional remedies, all of which are enforceable by law.

But to enjoy your Fundamental Rights, you have to remember your **Fundamental Duties** —to respect all our national symbols, to work for the unity of the country, to avoid violence and spread the message of peace, and to preserve our heritage, environment and public property.

The constitution describes India as a **Union of States**. That means the country is made up of several states, each with its own legislature and government and courts. But the states are all linked together and come under the central government.

Finally, the constitution introduces a **Parliamentary** form of government, and divides it into the legislative, executive and judicial branches. Each branch limits or checks the powers of the other two, so that no wing becomes too powerful, and they all work together.

What makes the constitution most special though? The fact that it puts the power in the hands of ordinary people like you and me!

# for Constitution

## THREE FOR THE COUNTRY

**The Legislative Branch**: The Lok Sabha or House of the People and the Rajya Sabha or Council of States are the two Houses of Parliament. Together they form the central legislature. The constitution grants the legislative branch the power to make the laws of the country.

**The Executive Branch**: The executive division is headed by the President, and includes the Vice President and a Council of Ministers led by the prime minister. According to the constitution, the laws can be passed only with the consent of the President. But the real executive power lies with the prime minister, and the President usually acts on his advice.

**The Judicial Branch**: The Supreme Court is the highest court in the country. Then, there are the high courts and lower courts like the district courts, all of which go to make up the judicial unit. The Chief Justice of the Supreme Court is its head.

Dr B.R. Ambedkar, *Father of the Indian Constitution*

## BORROWING THE BEST

When our leaders drafted the constitution, they decided that they wanted the best for the people, which is why they included the finest bits from the constitutions of so many other countries in it. That's why the Indian Constitution is often called 'a bag of borrowings'. While it was mainly influenced by the British Constitution, the concepts of liberty, equality and fraternity were taken from France, the idea of five year plans was taken from the USSR, and principles like the separation of powers among the major branches of government, the establishment of a supreme court, and the system of having a president as well as a prime minister were taken from the American Constitution. Influences of many other countries like Ireland, Japan, Germany and Canada can also be seen in our constitution.

## COOL CONSTITUTION

• **Dr B.R. Ambedkar**, independent India's first law minister, oversaw the drafting of the constitution. He is called the Father of the Indian Constitution.

• It is the longest written constitution of any country in the world, containing 444 articles in 22 parts, 12 schedules and 118 amendments.

• The Constitution of India was handwritten and calligraphed in both English and Hindi. It was not typeset or printed. The original copies are kept in special helium-filled cases in the Library of the Parliament of India.

• In 1950, the Constitution of India was signed by our first President, **Dr Rajendra Prasad**, our first prime minister, **Jawaharlal Nehru** and many others. Nehru was so thrilled to be the first one to sign the historic document that he did so without leaving enough space for the President's signature! The President then had to squeeze his signature in above Nehru's.

# for Crafts

**From earthenware and papercraft to leatherware and metalcraft, the sheer size and diversity of our country is best reflected in the array of exquisite crafts we have!**

## ELEGANT EARTHENWARE

The first earthen pot was believed to be a gift from the gods. When the gods and demons were churning the ocean for nectar, they had no vessel to collect it. So the celestial builder Vishwakarma quickly gathered some earth and crafted it into a pot!

Archaeological evidence shows us that the people of the Indus Valley Civilization knew how to make burnt clay bricks and even created colourful glazed beads. The distinctive **blue pottery** that we use even today was developed during the rule of the Delhi Sultanate. In the 19th century, it was believed to have been taken to Jaipur by Raja Ram Singh. The unique feature of Jaipur blue pottery is that it uses fuller's earth, not clay.

Tons of glazed earthenware is made in Uttar Pradesh too, of which **Khurja** is the oldest and most famous. Kashmiri potters coat their products with glaze in a style that makes it resemble batik. This unusual craftwork is sold along the Dal Lake and is called **Dal Lake pottery**.

The **Bankura horse** of Bengal and the **kudirai (horse) of Ayyanar** in Tamil Nadu are fine examples of terracotta work. In fact, a cluster of horses in Semakottai in Tamil Nadu is considered the largest terracotta sculpture in the world!

*Beautiful terracotta Bankura horses from Bengal*

*Colourful shadow puppets made of leather, from Andhra Pradesh*

## LUXE LEATHER

Leather is most widely used in India to make footwear of all shapes and sizes. The **open chappals** of Kolhapur in Maharashtra are best known. The better the quality of the leather, the more they are likely to squeak when they are new! The **mojris** and **jootis** of Rajasthan are made of cured leather and then decorated.

Andhra Pradesh has a history of painting on leather. Colourful leather puppets and lampshades are made in **Kalamkari** style, which look striking against the light. At Shantiniketan in West Bengal, Rabindranath Tagore encouraged craftsmen to work with leather. **Batik** on leather is a Bengal speciality and their cane moorahs with puffed leather seats are very popular.

Before we started using eco-unfriendly plastic bottles, liquids were mainly carried in leather containers. The **kopi** of Bikaner in Rajastan is a beautiful example of how camel skin can be stretched, hardened and then decorated to make a striking water bottle.

## for Crafts

WE HAVE A HISTORY OF CRAFT MAKING, NOT 'BEING CRAFTY'.

## CREATIVE CRAFTS

• Papier mache masks and dancing dolls are made all over India. But the papier mache work of Kashmir, known as **kari kamandari**, is different in that the paper is not pulped. It is pasted layer over layer to get the right thickness.

• Sculpting deities in stone (granite and soapstone) is a great South Indian tradition. The statue of **Bahubali** at Shravanabelagola in Karnataka is 57 feet high and is the tallest monolithic statue (a statue made from a single stone) in the world!

• Pathamadai in Tamil Nadu produces the finest mats in the country. Made from fine **korai grass** that grows locally, each light, foldable mat takes approximately 22 days to weave!

## MARVELLOUS METALCRAFT

The bronze statuette of the dancing girl of Mohenjodaro, the giant iron pillar next to the Qutub Minar, the burial urn at Adichanallur . . . all point to the fact that we had perfected various metal casting techniques eons ago.

**Brass temple bells** are a Gujarati speciality, and the one on Girnar Hill weighs 240 kg! The **brass plates** of Thanjavur in Tamil Nadu are well-known too. Alternating copper and silver sheets are encrusted on the brass plate, which usually depicts stories of Shiva or Vishnu. In fact, because of the number of complex techniques used to make this plate, it has been referred to as 'a dictionary of decorative methods'!

Most of our beautiful lamps are made of brass or bell metal—be it the stambha or pillar lamp, the **kuthuvillakku** or the five-wick lamp, the **vrindavan** or the garden lamp or the **deepalakshmi** or the lamp in the form of a woman holding a bowl.

Bronze icons are synonymous with Tamil Nadu and the greatest of them were made by the Cholas around the 10th century CE. The most well-known centre is at Swamimalai, where the striking **Nataraja** (Lord Shiva dancing the tandava) was created.

Persian metalworkers were believed to have been hired on contract and brought to Bidar in Karnataka, where they developed the unique art of inlaying intricate silver designs on darkened zinc—a craft which is known as **bidri**.

And the marvellous **metal mirror from Aranmula** in Kerala, is made of a copper-tin alloy. It is polished to such perfection that it reflects like glass!

*Metal is polished so perfectly that it reflects like glass in the Aranmula mirror from Kerala.*

# for Cricket

**Tens of thousands of people watching and cheering as two teams of 11 players each engage in a bat-and-ball game to score more runs than the other . . . Yes, we're talking of cricket, India's most popular and well-loved sport!**

## GIFTING A GAME

Whatever else the British gave us, they gave us the game of cricket. And since it came to us at a time when we were ruled by the British, we took to the game with a determination to beat them at their own game!

The first recorded instance of cricket being played in the subcontinent is of a match between the English sailors of the East India Company playing at Cambay, near **Baroda**, in 1721. The **Parsis** were the first Indians to play the game way back in 1848. They promoted the first cricket clubs in India, and in 1886 and 1888, organized the first ever overseas cricket tours by Indians. In the years that followed, they became so good at the game that they even defeated several teams of visiting English cricketers.

## MAKING CRICKET OUR OWN

India became a member of the 'elite cricketing club' in 1932, joining England, South Africa, New Zealand and the West Indies. India's first match in Lords against England in 1932 (under the captaincy of **C.K. Nayadu**) attracted a massive crowd of 24,000 people, including the King of England, who also happened to be the Emperor of India! It was played for three days. India lost the match by 158 runs.

India's first test victory over England came in Chennai in 1952, but it wasn't until 1971 when we won a test on English soil at the Oval and recorded a historic first ever series victory over the hosts, that we made it our own. From its early avatar as a gentleman's game and a symbol of English culture, cricket had moved on to become our unofficial national game.

After we won the World Cup for the first time in 1983, it was decided that India would host the next one in 1987, making us the first nation outside England to host a World Cup.

India's most popular sport, cricket

## CRICKET FOR EVERY SEASON AND REASON

Today, the Indian national cricket team plays every form of the game internationally—from **test cricket** to **one day internationals** to the **Twenty20** format. They also play in domestic competitions like the **Ranji Trophy** and the **Duleep Trophy**.

Besides this, gully cricket is a phenomenon unique to India, where children and adults alike play the game at any nook and corner available. In fact, Chennai is popularly known as the 'street cricket capital of the world'.

# for Cuisines

If there's one thing that unites Indians in every nook and corner of the country, it is our love for food. And why not, when we have delectable treats made to cater to every taste . . . and every waist!

## IT'S ALL A MATTER OF TASTE

According to an ancient Indian food theory, there are seven basic tastes or **rasas**: sweet, sour, salty, spicy, pungent, bitter and astringent. So a typical yummy Indian meal is a well balanced combination of these tastes. Dishes that accompany rice (the staple food of South India) or rotis (made from wheat, and the basic food of North India) are made keeping in mind how the rasas can be combined tastily. And, if any rasa is missing in the main meal, we always have condiments like pickles, chutneys, papads and raitas at arm's length!

Delicious Mughlai dishes like pilafs and kebabs have become an integral part of Indian cuisine.

INDIAN FOOD HAS ONLY ONE TASTE – YUMMY!

## A CONFLUENCE OF CUISINES

Every region in India has its own special cuisine, which is mainly influenced by the climate of the place, availability of fresh produce, religion, customs and beliefs. So if there are parathas and lassi in Punjab, there are kebabs and biriyanis in Uttar Pradesh, luchis and machher jhol in Bengal, kadhi and khichdi in Gujarat and dosa and sambar in Tamil Nadu!

## GHEE WITH GLEE

If there's one word synonymous with Indian food, it has got to be ghee. For most Indians, ghee is the purest form of milk, making it the best cooking medium. So whether it is our spicy food or our sweet treats, everything gets doused in generous dollops of ghee! Also, Indians believe that ghee, when eaten in the right proportion, cools the body. A story goes that when the priest in a temple was asked why Indians cook using ghee, he is supposed to have said, 'Anyone can cook in refined oil, but to cook in ghee, one ought to have attained moksha!'

What's more, we have happily opened our kitchens to invasions by the culinary traditions of every empire that ruled the country, be it the Mughals, the Portuguese or the English. So if matar paneer, aloo bhaji and chilly chicken have you drooling, thank the Portuguese for introducing paneer, potatoes and chillies to India! Perhaps the Mughal style of cooking has had the deepest influence on Indian cuisine. Besides rich gravies, pilafs and kebabs, the Mughals were also the people who introduced apricots, plums, peaches, melons, cherries and apples to India. And we have the British to thank for all the flavourful teas we drink.

# for Cuisines

## SWEET EVERYTHINGS

No Indian meal is complete without a sweet treat. Err . . . not a sweet, but hundreds of them actually, in every colour, shape, consistency and texture. Why do we love our sweets? Well, for the record, our gods are crazy about them! No pooja is complete without offering **bhoga** (sweets) to the gods, which are made with a pure heart and pure ghee, of course! And once they've been offered to the gods as prasad, they absolutely need to be distributed to the devotees, so that the blessings are transferred automatically.

Most Indian sweets have a base of milk, cream or condensed milk. Then, depending on what is being made, it is combined with ghee, sugar, chickpea flour or semolina wheat, almond, cashew or pistachio, coconut, cardamon, saffron and a host of other things. And because sweets are for special occasions, many are covered with a delicate layer of silver known as varkha.

From rosogollas, gulab jamuns, rasmalai and kheer, through laddoos, halwas and jalebis, to barfis, pedas and our very own desi kulfi icecream, the list of Indian sweetmeats is endless and delicious!

*Mithai to indulge every kind of sweet tooth*

## ONE FOR THE STREET

The quintessential Indian street food is **chaat**, a generic name for different kinds of tangy-spicy savoury treats. The word comes from the Hindi 'chaatna', which means to lick and from the Prakrit 'chattei', which translates to eating noisily with relish!

The original chaat is a mixture of potato pieces, small crisp pancakes made of fried flour, gram, yoghurt and a mix of spices. Today, there are as many varieties as there are Indians and the popular chaats include aloo tikkis, bhel puri, pani puri, papdi chaat and more! What gives chaat its yummy flavour? A special chaat masala, which is made by powdering different spices in particular combinations known only to the person making it.

NO, SILLY! YOU HAVE A *PAAN* AFTER MEALS!

## FUNKY FOOD FACTS

• In the 2010 national survey conducted by *Outlook* magazine, the **masala dosa** was voted our national dish and the **rosogolla** our national dessert!

• An Indian meal is considered done only when you chew a **paan** or betel leaves rolled with areca nuts.

• What is India's national drink? Coffee or tea? Well, India's tea growers did ask the government to declare tea as the national drink, but the government refused to promote one over the other. And, in any case, just because the mango was declared our national fruit, did we stop eating bananas and apples?

# for Dabbawala

Hungry kya? Then, dial a pizza, unless of course you live in Mumbai, where an efficient dabbawala will pick up your lunch box from home and deliver it to you right where you are!

## OUT OF THE BOX

The concept of the dabbawala (or lunch box delivery man) originated when the British were ruling India. Many British officers could not stomach the spicy local food, so a service was set up to fetch lunches from their homes to their workplaces. What started out as a small service soon grew into a super-efficient lunch delivery system, and today, approximately 4500 dabbawalas pick up about 1,75,000 lunches from homes and deliver them to students, workers and office-goers on every working day. At 12.30 p.m. on the dot. Served hot, of course!

## TIFFIN ON TIME

The dabbawala service originated in 1880. The commercial arm of this service was registered in 1968 as the **Mumbai Tiffin Box Suppliers Association**, and it provides efficient door-to-door services at nominal charges to this day.

How do the dabbawalas work? A collecting dabbawala, usually on bicycle, picks up tiffin boxes from homes between 7 a.m. and 9 a.m. The boxes are taken to a designated sorting place and then loaded on to Dabbawala Special Trains at the nearest railway station. A colour-coded marking on the tiffin box's handle identifies its owner and destination. At various stations, they are unloaded on to platforms and sorted again for area-wise distribution. A single tiffin box could change hands three to four times in the course of its daily journey! Finally, at destination stations, the boxes are handed over to a local dabbawalla, who delivers them. Once lunch is done, the whole process moves into reverse gear and the tiffin boxes return to their homes by 6 p.m.!

## BELIEVE IT OR NOT!

• According to an article in *Forbes* magazine, one mistake for every eight million deliveries is the norm in the unique dabbawala system. And this, with zero documentation and a barely literate workforce!

• The dabbawalas have never gone on strike right from when they came into existence in 1880. The only exception was made in 2011 when many of them headed off to support Anna Hazare in his anti-corruption campaign!

• Prince Charles, who wanted to see the dabbawala operations when he visited India, had to fit his schedule into theirs, since their timings were too precise to allow any alterations!

## for Dances

**Did you know that the first archaeological proof of human beings dancing comes from rock paintings done thousands of years ago on the walls of the Bhimbetka caves in Madhya Pradesh? Yes, dance is in our blood . . . and our feet!**

## A GIFT OF THE GODS

Like many Indian art forms, dance too has its origins in religion. The story in the *Natya Shastra* goes that the devas and asuras in heaven were constantly fighting for wealth and power. Tired with the non-stop fighting, the devas requested Lord Indra to come up with a means of entertainment that would soothe their eyes and ears. Lord Indra promptly went to Lord Brahma, the creator, and asked him to help them. Lord Brahma went into meditation. He took words from the Rigveda, gestures from the Yajurveda, music from the Samaveda and emotions from the Atharvaveda to create 'natya' or dance. Lord Brahma then asked Sage Bharata to write the *Natya Shastra*, a manual on the performing arts, which defines the practice of dance, drama and music, and whose guidelines are followed to this day.

The fact that so many of our gods and goddesses are represented dancing shows how the concept of dance is intrinsic to India. Shiva's cosmic dance, the tandava, Kali's dance of creation and destruction and Krishna's Rasalila with the gopikas are mentioned in Hindu mythology.

## IT'S A CLASSIC!

Classical dance in India is not limited to mere dance movements. It usually includes elements of singing and acting. In a sense, our dances are more like dance dramas, which enact stories from Hindu mythology. A dance is considered classical when it strictly follows the guidelines laid down in the *Natya Shastra*. The Sangeet Natak Akademi, India's premier academy for the performing arts, currently confers classical status on eight Indian dance styles: **Bharatanatyam** (Tamil Nadu), **Kathak** (Uttar Pradesh), **Kathakali** (Kerala), **Kuchipudi** (Andhra Pradesh), **Manipuri** (Manipur), **Mohiniyattam** (Kerala), **Odissi** (Odisha), and **Sattriya** (Assam).

*Bharatanatyam is well known for its graceful movements and sculpture-like poses.*

MIND YOUR STEP LADY!

WOOF!

for Dances

## ANYBODY CAN DANCE!

While classical dance is considered a higher art form defined by rules and performed in courts, temples and sabhas, folk dance is often said to be the simple dance of the common people as an expression of their daily work, rituals and everyday happenings.

Every state of India has its own folk and tribal dance forms and people can break into a jig for any number of reasons—be it to celebrate the birth of a child, to announce the arrival of different seasons, to observe a wedding ceremony or quite simply to express joy and happiness. Most folk dancers also sing while being accompanied by musicians on various instruments. Some of our popular folk dances include **bhangra**, **bihu**, **garba**, **gotipua**, **kalbelia** and **yakshagana**.

## FUNKY FACTS

• **Bharatanatyam** is considered to be a fire dance—the movements of an authentic Bharatanatyam dancer resemble a dancing flame.

• **Kathak** ankle bells are different from those of all other Indian dance styles—they are not fixed on to a pad or a strip of leather, but are individually woven along a thick string.

• The elaborate make-up in **Kathakali** is to distinguish characters as super beings from another world who are satvik or godlike, rajasik or heroic and tamasik or demonic.

• A distinctive feature of **Kuchipudi** is the tarangam, in which the dancer performs on the edges of a brass plate, sometimes also balancing a pot of water on the head.

• **Manipuri** dancers do not wear ankle bells in contrast to all other Indian dance forms and the dancer's feet never strike the ground hard.

• Women were never allowed to perform the Kathakali dance in Kerala, which is why **Mohiniyattam** was created as the feminine counterpart of Kathakali.

• In the **Gotipua** tradition of Odissi dance, young boys dress like women to dance in praise of Lord Jagannath and Lord Krishna.

• Traditionally, **Sattriya** was performed only by bhokots (male monks) in monasteries as a part of their daily rituals or to mark special festivals.

Dancers performing the lively bhangra

## for Delhi

**New Delhi, India's pulsating capital, is its third largest city and the second most used entry point into the country. Built on the banks of River Yamuna, the city is a beautiful blend of a historic past and a vibrant present. Don't dilly-dally . . . get to Delhi!**

## ONE CITY, TWO WORLDS

India's magnificent capital city encompasses two very different worlds within it. **Old Delhi**, which was once the capital of Islamic India, is a maze of narrow lanes dotted with imposing mosques, bustling bazaars and crumbling mansions. In contrast, spacious **New Delhi**, which was created by the British as the imperial capital of India, is full of tree-lined avenues, beautiful bungalows and stately government buildings. No other city possibly brings together old India and new India so seamlessly or reflects better the course of its life and thought down the ages.

## DELHI DELIGHTS

• Delhi is one of the greenest cities in the world with a green cover of almost 20 per cent. **Delhi Ridge** is the city's largest forest and is often called its 'green lungs'. The ridge makes Delhi the world's second bird-rich capital city after Nairobi in Kenya.

• The **Delhi Transport Corporation** operates the world's largest fleet of environment-friendly CNG buses.

• Delhi is a city of museums. The **National Museum**, **Nehru Museum**, and **Crafts Museum** have excellent collections. There's also a **Metro Museum**, which is the world's first museum to be located inside a working metro station. And yes, Delhi has an **International Toilet Museum** too!

• Delhi has three UNESCO World Heritage Sites: the **Red Fort** built by Shah Jahan, the **Qutub Minar** built by Qutb-ud-din Aibak and **Humayun's Tomb** built by Bega Begum, his widow. The city as a whole has been trying to claim a position on the World Heritage List for a few years now.

*The magnificent Humayun's Tomb, built of red sandstone, represented a building tradition that inspired the construction of the Taj Mahal a century later.*

## for Delhi

# A TALE OF EIGHT CITIES

Delhi has been the seat of power for about a millennium and several rulers and their kingdoms flourished here. Down the ages, the city was built, destroyed and then rebuilt by emperors, and it has the unique distinction of being India's capital longer than any other city. In fact, an ancient legend goes thus: 'he who rules Delhi, rules India'.

It is believed that at least eight Delhis existed before the present city of New Delhi was built. The earliest reference to Delhi is found in the Mahabharata. The city is believed to be the site of **Indraprastha**, the legendary capital of the Pandavas. In 736 CE Anang Pal of the Tomara dynasty founded the first city of **Lal Kot** which was renamed **Qila Rai Pithora** by the Chauhans, when they conquered it.

The Chauhans were defeated in 1192 CE by the Afghan invader Muhammad Ghori, and with his rule began the Muslim dominance of India, which lasted for the next 600 years. His commander Qutub-ud-din Aibak became the first Sultan of Delhi and founded the second

city of **Mehrauli**. **Siri** was built around 1303 CE during the rule of Ala-ud-din Khilji of the Delhi Sultanate. Ghiyas-ud-din Tughlaq, the founder of the Tughlaq dynasty, built **Tughlaqabad** in 1321 CE. The Delhi Sultanate reached its greatest extent under Muhammad bin Tughlaq, who shifted his capital to Daulatabad in Maharashtra. But by moving away from Delhi, he lost control of the north and was forced to return to the city. Tughlaq built the fortified city of **Jahanpanah** in 1327 CE on his return to restore order. Firoze Shah Tughlaq was a more sensible ruler than his father and he created the next city of Delhi, **Ferozabad** or Firoze Shah Kotla as it is known today.

In 1526 CE, a new chapter in Delhi's history was written when Babar defeated Ibrahim Lodhi and established the Mughal dynasty. Babar's son Humayun was ousted by Sher Shah Suri in 1540 CE. He set up another city called **Shergarh** on the ruins of Dinpanah that Humayun had built. Mughal glory was restored when Shah Jahan came to power and built **Shahjahanabad** in 1648 CE.

The Mughal dynasty pretty much came to an end in 1803 CE with the growth of British power in India. On 12 December 1911, at the historic Delhi Durbar, Emperor George V proclaimed the shifting of the capital of India from Calcutta to Delhi. **New Delhi** was built as the glittering capital of British India by architects Edwin Lutyens and Herbert Baker and inaugurated on 13 February 1931.

WHAT? DID YOU SAY A1 GRADES? ABHI DILLI DOOR HAI!

# DELHI IN A PHRASE

Ever heard someone saying 'abhi Dilli door hai' (Delhi is still far off) while referring to a job that's far from being completed? Well, there's an interesting story behind it. The emperor Ala-ud-din Khilji wanted the eminent Sufi saint Hazrat Nizamuddin Auliya to help him run his kingdom. But the saint refused. When the king insisted, the Hazrat said that he would leave Delhi and go away. Ala-ud-din's son Qutb-ud-din too kept pestering the saint, but when he continued to refuse, Qutb-ud-din ordered the Hazrat to leave Delhi before he returned from a conquest. Hearing this, the Hazrat is believed to have said, 'abhi Dilli door hai'. Qutb-ud-din died before he reached Delhi! And the phrase became so popular that it is used even today to refer to a task or journey that has a long way to go before it gets done.

## for Elections

**Why do we hold elections? Because we are a democracy and we believe that people should have a chance to choose their representatives in the government and determine the political future of the country.**

*Parliament House is the place from which the ruling party governs our country.*

## WE ARE A DEMOCRACY

India is the world's largest democracy. The word 'democracy' derives from a combination of the Greek words 'demos' (people) and 'kratos' (rule), which together means the 'rule of the people'. So, a democracy is a form of government in which the people, either directly or indirectly, take part in governing the country. And how does this happen? Through elections, of course. In order to conduct elections, a vast country like India is divided into several constituencies. When polls are held once every five years, each constituency elects one candidate who gets one seat in the government.

IT IS THE POLITICIANS WHO TURN THE SYSTEM INTO A DEMOCRAZY!

## WHY ARE ELECTIONS HELD?

India is a Parliamentary democracy, which means the government is formed by the political party that has the maximum number of elected representatives in Parliament. What does that mean? Well, in a democracy, people make laws and govern themselves. But millions of us cannot sit together and do that, can we? So we elect people who represent us in Parliament and make laws. That makes our country a Parliamentary democracy.

The Parliament is our highest governing body and consists of the President of India, the Lok Sabha and the Rajya Sabha. The Lok Sabha or the House of the People has 543 members, who are voted directly by the people for a term of five years. These elected members represent Parliamentary constituencies across the country. The Rajya Sabha or the Council of States has 245 members, of which 233 are elected indirectly by the state legislatures for a term of six years. The remaining 12 members are nominated by the President for their contributions to art, literature, science **and** social services.

So elections are important because that's how we get a chance to choose all these people are our representatives.

# for Elections

## YOUR VOTE COUNTS

In India, citizens who are 18 or older can vote. It's one person, one vote. And you get to vote irrespective of whether you're rich or poor, man or woman, religious or atheistic . . . and that's what we call **universal adult suffrage**.

An estimated 61 crore Indians voted in the 2019 general elections to the 17th Lok Sabha. That's a number larger than the electorate of the European Union and United States put together, making it the largest democratic election in the world to date!

*Young voters display their inked fingers after casting votes during an election.*

## YOUR VOTE IS TOP SECRET

Elections are conducted by the **Election Commission**, which is an independent body that supervises the polling procedure. In India, voting is by secret ballot. That means, at the polling station, you mark the ballot paper with a rubber stamp near the symbol of the candidate of your choice inside a screened compartment where no one can see whom you're voting for. Of course, we have electronic voting machines nowadays, where you just press a button to pick the candidate of your choice. The 2009 general elections were conducted completely using electronic voting machines (EVMs), and approximately 14 lakh of them were used. Ten years later, in the 2019 elections, nearly 4 million EVMs were used for polling!

## BELIEVE IT OR NOT!

• Over a million polling stations were set up by the Election Commission for the 2019 general elections. At a height of 15,256 feet, the polling station set up in Tashigang, Himachal Pradesh, was the highest in the world.

• An election team had to travel 35 km just so the only resident of the remote Gir National Forest in Gujarat could vote. The temple priest got his own polling station, complete with an EVM!

• After having completely shifted to EVMs more than a decade ago, the Election Commission came close to returning to paper ballots in one small constituency: Nizamabad in Telangana. A whopping 185 candidates filed nominations here, while an EVM is designed to accommodate a maximum of 64 candidates. How did they solve this problem? Well, 12 big-sized EVMs, each accommodating the names and party symbols of 16 candidates, were placed in an L-shaped format in each of the 1778 polling booths here!

ALL RIGHT VOTERS, TURN TO *PAGE 24* TO GO TO THE SYMBOL OF *MY* POLITICAL PARTY!

BALLOT

# E

## for Emperors

For centuries, many great men ruled India using their wisdom, military might, love for arts and culture and the ability to ensure the welfare of their people. They were much more than mere rulers of their kingdoms. They were great emperors who shaped the course of our history.

## THE KING WHO SAID NO TO WAR

### Ashoka (304–232 BCE)

By the time Ashoka came to the throne in 272 BCE, almost all of India was part of the Mauryan Empire. Except one tiny kingdom called Kalinga, which was of vital strategic importance because it was the access point to various land and sea routes to South India. So what did Ashoka do? He waged a long and bloody war against Kalinga, in which lakhs of people died.

Shocked by the devastation he had caused, Ashoka took some time off to think about what he could do to make amends. It was at this time that the non-violence preached by Buddhism appealed to him. So he became a Buddhist and swore never to go to war again. Of course this didn't mean he would not defend his kingdom if it was in danger—it only meant that he would never attack first!

I TOO HAVE BEGUN TO PRACTICE *NON-VIOLENCE*. I DON'T FIGHT WITH MY MATHS PROBLEMS ANY MORE.

## AMAZING ASHOKA

When India become independent, it was time to choose a national emblem to represent the country. People felt that Ashoka's principles of non-violence and religious tolerance were still valid. That's why the four lions standing back to back on one of Ashoka's pillars was chosen as our national symbol.

## AN EMPEROR PAR EXCELLENCE

### Akbar (1542–1605 CE)

Akbar was the greatest Mughal emperor to rule India. While all the Mughal kings before him hated the heat of Delhi and yearned for the cool climes of Kabul, Akbar was the first ruler to truly consider India his home.

He established a sprawling kingdom through military conquest. However, he was also the most religiously tolerant of all the Mughal emperors. He encouraged people in his kingdom to follow their own religion, and in fact even founded a brand-new one called Din-i-Ilahi, which combined the best tenets of all religions. In 1575, he constructed the Ibadat Khana or House of Worship within the walled city of Fatehpur Sikri where he often hosted scholars from various faiths. Akbar's court was also renowned for his nine well-known courtiers called the Navaratnas.

IF AKBAR WAS HERE NOW, I COULD HAVE EASILY BEATEN HIM IN *SCRABBLE!*

## AWESOME AKBAR

You know that Akbar was one of our greatest kings, but did you know that he was also a warrior, general, artist, blacksmith, carpenter, animal trainer (he had thousands of cheetahs and trained them himself!), lacemaker and theologian? And this despite not knowing how to read or write!

# for Emperors

## SUPER SHIVAJI

From a small contingent of 2000 soldiers that he inherited from his father, Shivaji created an army of 1,00,000 soldiers, who used his guerrilla warfare methods and won dozens of battles. In fact, his tactic of disappearing into the Western Ghats with his soldiers and springing surprise attacks on his enemy was so stealthy that Aurangazeb called him a 'mountain rat'!

*A portrait of the Maratha warrior and emperor, Shivaji*

## THE MAHARAJA OF MILITARY MANOEUVRES

### Shivaji (1627?–1680 CE)

Shivaji was one of the most enigmatic kings of India. Opinions about Shivaji are divided between him being a national hero who successfully resisted the Mughals and him being a mere Maratha warrior who established an empire in western India. Either way, the fact is that he was a master military planner. He built a strong navy and guarded his kingdom's coastline by setting up many sea forts. In fact his navy was so powerful that it stood its own against the Portuguese, Dutch and British fleets.

Shivaji was a pioneer of many military strategies. He had a mobile light infantry and cavalry excelling in commando tactics, a well-organized spy and intelligence network, and an army of trained peasants who worked as part-time soldiers. He also made novel use of traditional weapons like the tiger claw! His most innovative tactic, however, was using guerrilla warfare and making sudden attacks that left his opponents dazed and defeated.

I HEARD SOME TALK ABOUT *PORRIDGE*. HAS THE WAR ENDED?

## FUNKY ROYAL FACTS

• As a child, whenever **Chandragupta Maurya** ate hot porridge, his mother advised him to eat from the sides first. Years later, he used this as military strategy. He attacked places from their fringes and then moved inside, thus conquering many territories!

• The Mughal emperor **Babar** was believed to be so strong and fit that he could run on a parapet carrying one man under each of his arms!

• It is said that **Mahbub Ali Pasha**, the 6th Nizam of Hyderabad, never wore an outfit twice. His dressing room had the world's longest wardrobe, which was 240 feet long!

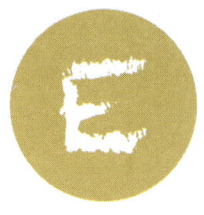

# for Energy

It is a universally accepted fact that economic development and energy consumption go hand in hand. The growth of an economy hinges on the availability of cost-effective energy much like the level of economic development is dependent on the energy demand. So how is India coping?

## ENERGIZING INDIA

About 70 per cent of India's energy generation capacity is from fossil fuels like **coal**, **crude oil** and **natural gas**. Coal is our most important source to meet domestic energy needs and it accounts for 40 per cent of the country's total energy supplies. Crude oil and natural gas take care of 24 per cent and 6 per cent of our energy requirements, respectively.

## WHY DO WE NEED SO MUCH ENERGY?

We need energy primarily to provide electricity to India. In recent times, we have moved faster than any other country in the world to deliver electricity to people, extending our electricity grids to reach over 24 million more people each year since 1990.

Despite our soaring energy needs, India has one of the lowest per capita rates of consumption of power in the world—1181 units as compared to a world average of 2674 units. This is nothing compared with the rates of countries like Canada (14,930 units) and USA (12,071 units). That notwithstanding, we still do not have enough fossil fuels to meet our growing energy demands.

## RENEW IT RIGHT

• India was the first country in the world to set up a ministry of non-conventional energy resources, in the early 1980s. But we haven't really tapped into our potential completely. Our main sources of renewable energy are solar power, wind power and biomass material.

• Supported by the United Nations Environment Programme, we have put in place the **Indian Solar Loan Programme**, which is a consumer financing scheme to set up solar powered homes, particularly in rural areas where electricity hasn't yet reached.

• The development of **wind power** in India began in the 1990s, and has significantly increased in the last few years. Today, we have the 5th largest installed wind power capacity.

• India produces a huge quantity of **biomass** material through its agricultural, agro-industrial and forestry operations. It is estimated that the biomass resources of our country can actually replace present consumption of all fossil fuels if used productively.

• There are 232 million cattle in the country. If one-third of the dung produced annually by these cattle is available for **biogas** production and for recycling as farm manure, 12 million biogas plants can be installed!

## for Epics

The Ramayana and the Mahabharata, originally written in Sanskrit and then translated into several languages, are some of the oldest surviving epic poems on earth! These timeless poems form a part of our rich literary tradition and have influenced almost every story written in India thereafter!

## HEY RAMA!

The word 'Ramayana' literally means the march (ayana) of Rama. Rama, the hero of the story, is an avatar of Lord Vishnu. He makes a journey in search of human values. In narrating his journey, the tale describes different relationships, portraying characters like the ideal father, the ideal brother, the ideal wife and the ideal king.

The Ramayana consists of 24,000 rhyming couplets called shlokas which are written in a complex 32-syllable metre called anustubh. These verses are grouped into individual chapters called sargas, which narrate specific events in the story. The sargas are collected into books called kandas. There are seven kandas in all: the Bal Kanda (Rama's childhood), the Ayodhya Kanda (Rama's life in Ayodhya till his banishment), the Aranya Kanda (Rama's life in the forest and Sita's abduction by Ravana), the Kishkindha Kanda (Rama's stay at Kishkindha, the capital of the monkey-king, Sugriva), the Sundara Kanda (Rama's journey to Sri Lanka), the Yuddha Kanda or Lanka Kanda (Rama's battle with Ravana and return to Ayodhya with Sita) and the Uttara Kanda (Rama's life in Ayodhya as king, the birth of his two sons, Sita's test of innocence and return to earth and Rama's demise).

Phew, surely this is one long story that cannot really be cut short!

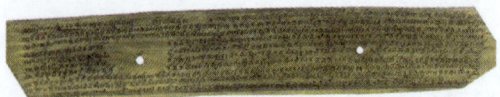

*A painting of Valmiki penning the Ramayana*

## VALMIKI, WHO?

Valmiki, the author of the Ramayana, is respected as the Adi Kavi or First Poet, who wrote the first shloka in Sanskrit poetry. So was he a man of high learning? On the contrary, he was Daku Ratnakar, a fearsome thief and a cruel hunter!

One day, Ratnakar killed a deer in the forest right where some rishis were performing a yagna. When they told him that he would be cursed by the gods, he regretted what he had done and asked the sages what he could do to atone for his mistake. The rishis told him to sit under a sal tree and recite Rama's name repeatedly till they finished their prayers. Unfortunately, they completely forgot about him and left once their yagna was done. Many months later, when Sage Narada was passing by the same area, he saw the robber still chanting the lord's name. Narada shook him out of his meditation, blessed him and told him to devote the rest of his life to Rama. Since a 'valmika' or an anthill had grown over his body during his long penance, Daku Ratnakar came to be known as Valmiki!

## for Epics

### A MAHA STORY

The Mahabharata, which translates to 'the great tale of the Bharata dynasty' is the longest Sanskrit epic in the world. Its longest version consists of over 1,00,000 shlokas, which roughly means 2,00,000 individual verse lines, and many long prose passages, all of which are grouped under 18 parvas or books. With a word count of about 1.8 million the Mahabharata is seven times the length of the Iliad and the Odyssey put together and about four times the length of the Ramayana!

Besides narrating the epic story of the battle between the Kauravas and Pandavas for the throne of Hastinapur, other literary and religious works like the Bhagavad Gita, the story of Damayanti, an abbreviated version of the Ramayana, and the tale of Rishyasringa are all part of the Mahabharata!

A painting of Lord Krishna as the charioteer who leads Arjuna to the Kurukshetra War.

### PEN PALS FROM LONG AGO

The Mahabharata is believed to have been written by Sage Vyasa, who incidentally also plays an important role in the story. It is said that Lord Brahma suggested that Vyasa approach Lord Ganesha to pen the story. On being asked, Ganesha immediately agreed, but on one condition—that Sage Vyasa should never pause in his recitation. Well, Vyasa had an ace up his sleeve too. He said that that was fine as long as Ganesha understood what was being narrated before jotting it down!

The story goes that Ganesha's quill broke while he was writing. So he broke off one of his tusks and used it to continue writing the epic tale! That's why he is called Ekadanta, the lord with a single tusk.

The Mahabharata is believed to have been composed in a cave near Mana village in present-day Uttarakhand. Located 3 km from Badrinath, the cave is popularly known as **Ganesh Gufa**.

## for Festivals

**Festivals in India are celebrated for every reason and season, for every religion and region, for every legend and myth . . . which is why we are often called the Land of Festivals!**

### FESTIVAL FUNDA

1 January is the first day of the year and 31 December the last according to the solar calendar. But we Indians are mostly lunar people, which means the moon determines everything that happens in our life, especially our festivals. Whether the moon waxes or wanes, whether it is going to be seen at all . . . decides on what day of the month a festival is going to be celebrated and how!

Here's a pick of one major festival that happens every month. However, depending on the cycle of the moon, these festivals can sometimes shift months, so make sure you watch that calendar!

### JOLLY JANUARY

Get set to join the **Makara Sankranti** festivities all over India. According to the lunar calendar, the sun moves from the Tropic of Cancer to the Tropic of Capricorn on this day. In places like Gujarat and Rajasthan, people believe it is the day the direction of the winds change, which is why they celebrate by flying kites of all shapes, sizes and colours!

Makara Sankranti is also a harvest festival that marks the end of winter. If you're in Punjab, the festival is celebrated as **Lohri**, in Karnataka as **Sankranti**, in Assam as **Magh Bihu**, and in Tamil Nadu as **Pongal**. By the way, make sure you have a bath on Makara Sankranti. There's a belief that you'll be born a donkey the next time around if you don't!

*Colourful kites fly high in the sky during Uttarayan (Makara Sankranti) in Gujarat.*

### FESTIVE FEBRUARY

It's **Maha Shivaratri** this month, the most important day of the year for devotees of Shiva. The story goes that the gods and the demons churned the ocean to acquire the nectar that would make them immortal. During the churning, a pitcher of poison strong enough to destroy the world was tossed up along with the nectar! The terrified gods and demons prayed to Lord Shiva, who simply drank up the poison and saved the world. Enough reason to thank the lord and worship his idol with milk, water and honey, don't you think?

# for Festivals

## MERRY MARCH

Come March and it is time to bring out those colours, for **Holi** is just round the corner! Squirt friends and family with gulal of all colours from pichkaris of all shapes. Dig into mouth-watering goodies like gujiya, malpua and puran poli. And, if you want to know why you can get to be messy and naughty and still be treated to all these delicacies, well, that's because Holi is the festival which welcomes spring. It also celebrates the victory of good over evil by reminding us of the story of Holika, who, at the order of the powerful demon king Hiranyakashipu, entered a blazing fire, taking the king's son Prahalad with her. Holika was burnt to ashes while Prahalad remained unhurt because of his devotion to Lord Vishnu. So, even now, bonfires are lit during Holi to celebrate this victory!

## AWESOME APRIL

While the world celebrates New Year in January, most parts of India welcome the New Year right in the middle of April! In Punjab, **Baisakhi** rings in the New Year with thanksgiving prayers for a good harvest of rabi crops. Men dance the energetic bhangra and women the lively gidda.

In Assam, **Bohag Bihu** combines the New Year, the spring festival and festivities to welcome the north-west winds which bring the rain-bearing clouds. In nearby Bengal, **Naba Barsha** is celebrated by drawing beautiful rangolis in front of the house to usher in wealth and prosperity. And down south, Tamil Nadu greets the New Year as **Puthandu**, while Andhra Pradesh and Karnataka observe **Ugadi** and Kerala, **Vishu**.

## MARVELLOUS MAY

**Buddha Jayanti** or **Buddha Purnima** is one of the most significant days on the Buddhist calendar. It falls on a full moon day in May and celebrates the birth of Prince Siddhartha under a tree in Lumbini, Nepal. Buddhists in Bodh Gaya, Sarnath, Ladakh and other parts of India worship Lord Buddha with flowers, incense sticks and candles. In keeping with the Buddha's teachings of non-violence, caged animals and birds are freed on this day.

*A colourful mask dance during the Hemis festival in Ladakh*

## JOYOUS JUNE

Get to the **Hemis Gompa**, India's oldest and biggest monastery in Ladakh in June, for this is where the colourful two-day Mela Hemis Gompa festival takes place to celebrate the birth anniversary of Guru Padmasambhava, the founder of Lamaism (an offshoot of Buddhism). The festival is truly a grand spectacle because lamas wearing colourful masks and elaborate costumes dance to the accompaniment of unwieldy trumpets, cymbals, drums and long horns! Every 12 years, in the Tibetan Year of the Monkey, a two-storey high, richly embroidered thangka painting depicting Guru Padmasambhava is displayed. 2004 was when this happened last, so book those tickets for 2016!

## for Festivals

## JUBILANT JULY

One of India's greatest annual festivals, the **Rath Yatra** or Chariot Festival, takes place in the seaside town of Puri in Orissa. Legend has it that King Indradyumna built a temple for Lord Jagannath, Balabhadra and their sister Subhadra in Puri. Vishwakarma, the architect of the gods, agreed to carve the images of the deities out of wood, but left them incomplete. Once a year, these unfinished wooden images are brought out of the temple and carried in gigantic chariots or rathas through the streets of Puri to Gundicha Bari about 4 km away. The journey takes over 24 hours simply because lakhs of devotees join the procession! The gods stay at Gundicha Bari for a week before returning to their own temple. On the way back, they stop at the Mausi Maa Temple (their aunt's home) to eat some poda pitha, which is Jagannath's favourite kind of pancake!

The English word 'juggernaut' comes from the huge chariots of Lord Jagannath that are pulled during the Puri Rath Yatra.

## AUSPICIOUS AUGUST

For Muslims, Ramadan is a holy month of fasting and prayer. And at the end of the month falls one of their most important festivals, **Eid al-Fitr** or the Festival of Fast Breaking. Fasting, according to Islamic belief, helps in inculcating self-control, which is a way of getting closer to Allah. But once the fasting ends, the celebrations and feasting begin! Nawabi biriyanis, delicious kormas, sweet seviyan and phirni . . . the list of goodies is endless. However, one important Id tradition that has to be followed amidst all the feasting and merry-making is to give alms to the less fortunate.

I STILL CAN'T FIGURE OUT HOW SNAKES CAN ROW BOATS...

GRRR

## SPLENDID SEPTEMBER

Let's go down south this month to celebrate **Onam**, the ten-day state festival of Kerala. Onam recalls the story of the proud asura king Mahabali, who created a prosperous kingdom in Kerala. Lord Vishnu as Vamana comes down to earth to crush his pride. He takes away everything that belongs to the king in three steps and Mahabali is pushed down to the netherworld. However, pleased with the king for letting him complete his three steps, Vishnu allows him to return to earth once a year to visit his kingdom. That's the day Kerala celebrates as Onam. They welcome their king back with beautiful pookkalams or rangolis of flowers, a procession of decorated elephants and an action-packed snake boat race! On the fourth day of Onam, which is called Nalaam Onam, dancers painted to look like tigers and hunters perform the amazing Puli Kali or tiger dance to the beats of many percussion instruments.

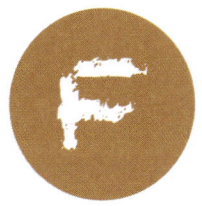

# for Festivals

Effigies of demon kings being burnt at the Kota mela.

## OPULENT OCTOBER

**Dussehra** or **Navaratri** too celebrates the victory of good over evil. While almost every part of India observes the festival, the top three spots are Kota (Rajasthan), Kolkata (West Bengal) and Mysore (Karnataka). At a colourful mela in Kota, effigies are made of the demon kings Ravana, Kumbhakarana and Meghnad, which are over 70 feet tall, and filled with firecrackers. On Vijayadashami day, which is the last day of Dussehra, a young child dressed as Lord Rama shoots an arrow of fire at the demons and they explode high into the night sky!

In Kolkata, the highlight of the festival is **Durga Puja**. Every neighbourhood puts up a splendidly decorated image of Durga destroying the buffalo-headed demon, Mahishasura, who is a symbol of ignorance. Huge crowds attend the festivities to pray, sing, eat and make merry.

In Mysore, the traditional Dussehra procession sees the idol of Goddess Chamundeshwari (who killed the demon Mahishasura) placed in a golden howdah atop a lavishly decorated elephant and taken from Mysore Palace to Bannimantap, where a spectacular torch-light parade and fireworks show takes place.

## NOISY NOVEMBER

When can you see Hindus, Sikhs, Buddhists, Jains and others happily celebrating one festival? During **Diwali**, of course! Hindus celebrate the festival to mark the homecoming of Lord Rama to Ayodhya after he killed Ravana. People were so happy that they lit thousands of lamps and made it the brightest night of the year. Sikhs celebrate the festival to commemorate the release of Guru Hargobind Singh from prison. He is believed to have gone straight to the Golden Temple afterwards, where people welcomed him with lit lamps. The Jains believe that Mahavira attained enlightenment on this day, while the Buddhists honour King Ashoka, who had converted to Buddhism on this day.

Diwali comes from the Sanskrit word 'Deepavali,' meaning row of lights, which are lit to honour Lakshmi, Goddess of Wealth, and to celebrate the victory of light over darkness. And the fun part? Exchanging gifts, goodies, good wishes and gupshup, of course!

WE TAKE UNITY IN DIVERSITY VERY SERIOUSLY!

## DELIGHTFUL DECEMBER

December can only mean one thing . . . the season of peace, goodwill, love and Santa! On 25 December, Christians celebrate the birth of Jesus Christ. According to legend, the Three Wise Men from the East, guided by the Star of Bethlehem, visited baby Jesus and brought him presents. So it became a custom to share goodies and gifts with family and friends and the poor during **Christmas**.

In India, instead of the traditional Christmas tree, sometimes a banana or mango tree is decorated. And Santa Claus delivers presents to children from his horse cart!

## for Forts

**High walls surrounded by moats, secret passageways and hidden ammunition chambers . . . India's fabulous forts are synonymous with heroic battles, tales of valour and spy stories!**

## THE BEST IN INDIA

Of the hundreds of formidable forts that have been built in India, two have been recognized by UNESCO as World Heritage Sites.

The **Lal Qila** or the **Red Fort** in Delhi is one of the most magnificent monuments of the Mughal era. It was built by Shah Jahan in 1639 CE on the banks of the River Yamuna. Its red sandstone walls, which rise 108 feet high, once kept fierce invaders away. Today, it keeps the hurly-burly of Old Delhi at bay! The Red Fort is the site from where the prime minister of India addresses the nation on 15 August.

The foundation stone for the impressive **Agra Fort** was laid by Akbar in 1565 CE. It took eight years to complete. Built like a walled city, the grand edifice grew to symbolize the might of the Mughal empire. The fort has a formidable appearance with four gateways and vast double walls that are 70 feet high and 2.5 km in length. It is said that the stones from which the walls are made are so well-joined that not even a strand of hair can pass through them!

FORTUNATELY FOR THEM, THEY HAD THE BEST ARCHITECTS!

## OLD IS GOLD

Located 20 km from Dharamsala in Himachal Pradesh, the **Kangra Fort** finds mention in the war records of Alexander the Great, making it the oldest fort in India. It was built by the Rajputs of Kangra, then captured by Mahmud of Ghazni, Muhammad bin Tughlaq, Jahangir and Raja Sansar Chand by turns before Maharaja Ranjit Singh annexed it and passed it on to the British. This gives the fort the unique distinction of being occupied by Hindus, Muslims, Sikhs and Christians across time!

## FASCINATING FORTS

• The **Golconda Fort** in Hyderabad has a remarkable echoing entrance hall. It is constructed in such a way that the guards at the entrance could notify the staff on the top of the fort (where the king's palace was) about the arrival of visitors by clapping their hands! The sound would get deflected by various structures and echo all the way to the top!

• The exquisite **Gwalior Fort** in Madhya Pradesh was described by the Mughal emperor Babar as 'the pearl in the necklace of the forts of Hind'. It occupies a unique position in history as the place which has the first ever written record of zero in India. A tablet describing the establishment of a small temple in the 9th century on the eastern side of the fort refers to shunya or zero in Sanskrit.

The Golconda Fort is built on a granite hill that is 400 feet high.

# F

## for Freedom Fighters

Many brave men and women played a key role in our fight for independence. They inspired the masses to join the freedom struggle, and through their collective efforts, made India a free country.

## THREE FOR FREEDOM

Sometime in the early 1900s, the Congress was divided into two groups—those who wanted to win freedom through peaceful, constitutional means (called the moderates) and those that preferred radical, revolutionary methods to get rid of the British (called the extremists). The extremists were represented by the popular Lal-Bal-Pal trio of **Lala Lajpat Rai**, **Bal Gangadhar Tilak** and **Bipin Chandra Pal**. All three of them advocated the Swadeshi movement and urged Indians to boycott the use of imported items. 'Swaraj is my birthright and I shall have it!' thundered Bal Gangadhar Tilak, as the trio mobilized Indians across the country to participate in strikes and boycotts that eventually ended British domination over India.

The Lal-Bal-Pal trio who propagated the Swadeshi movement in India

One of India's greatest freedom fighters, Shaheed Bhagat Singh

## MARTYRS TO A CAUSE

One of the greatest revolutionaries of the Indian Independence movement was young **Bhagat Singh**. He was born on 28 September 1907. As a student, he witnessed the brutal incident of Lala Lajpat Rai being beaten up by Police Chief James Scott for protesting against the Simon Commission. Lajpat Rai eventually succumbed to his injuries. In retaliation Bhagat Singh joined hands with other revolutionaries like **Sukhdev**, **Rajguru, Batukeshwar Dutt** and **Chandrashekar Azad** and plotted to kill Scott. However, Bhagat Singh accidentally ended up shooting Assistant Superintendent of Police John Saunders, mistaking him for Scott. The British immediately imposed the Defence of India Act 1915, which gave the police a free hand to curb revolutionary activities. Bhagat Singh and Batukeshwar Dutt then bombed the Central Legislative Assembly in Delhi on 8 April 1929, shouting slogans of 'Inquilab Zindabad'. For their radical activities, Bhagat Singh, Rajguru and Sukhdev were hanged on 23 March 1931.

It is said that no magistrate was willing to supervise Bhagat Singh's hanging. So, the execution was authorized by an honorary judge, who signed the three death warrants. Once the martyrs were hanged, the authorities broke the rear wall of the jail and secretly cremated the bodies in the dark of the night. Bhagat Singh was only 24 at the time of his execution.

## for Freedom Fighters

## AGENTS OF CHANGE

While many freedom fighters battled the British politically, some tackled social issues to help make India a truly modern nation. **Raja Ram Mohan Roy** worked tirelessly to eradicate the cruel practices of dowry, sati and child marriage through the Brahmo Samaj. **Ishwar Chandra Vidyasagar** took up the cause of widow remarriage and the education of women. **Dayanand Saraswati** founded the Arya Samaj to do away with the evils of the caste system and the oppressive customs of Hinduism, while **Dr B.R. Ambedkar** fought for social justice by working tirelessly to root out untouchability from India.

INDIA HAS ITS OWN *JUSTICE LEAGUE?* PERFECT!

## LADIES LEAD THE WAY

Many women in India were staunch patriots and participated actively in the freedom struggle.

**Sarojini Naidu** devoted her life to the cause of the empowerment of women. She was a great admirer of Gandhiji and followed his principles. In 1925, she was elected as the first female president of the India National Congress. In 1942, she was arrested during the Quit India movement and was jailed for 21 months along with Gandhiji and other leaders. She was the first woman to become governor of an Indian state (Uttar Pradesh) after India became independent.

**Sucheta Kriplani** came to the forefront during the Quit India Movement. She actively worked with Mahatma Gandhi during the riots following Partition. She was one of the few women who were elected to the Constituent Assembly and the first woman to serve as chief minister of a state (Uttar Pradesh) in independent India.

**Vijaya Lakshmi Pandit**, Jawaharlal Nehru's sister, was inspired by Sarojini Naidu to join the nationalist movement. Vijaya Lakshmi took part in the Non-Cooperation and Civil Disobedience movements. She was the first woman to become president of the United Nations General Assembly after we won our independence.

**Annie Besant** was a prominent British women's rights activist. She first visited India in 1893 and later settled here, becoming involved in the Indian nationalist movement. She was interested in Theosophy, a religious movement founded in 1875 based on Hindu ideas of karma and reincarnation. In 1916, Besant established the Indian Home Rule League and campaigned tirelessly for democracy in India.

**Dr Lakshmi Sahgal** joined the Indian National Army when she relocated to Singapore in 1940. When Subhas Chandra Bose arrived in Singapore in 1943, Lakshmi requested a meeting with him, having heard that he was keen to draft women into the INA. After a five-hour interview, she was given the opportunity to set up a separate women's regiment, the first of its kind in Asia. The regiment went on to be called the Rani of Jhansi regiment and she came to be known as Captain Lakshmi.

*Captain Lakshmi Sahgal, who set up the first women's regiment of the Indian National Army*

# for Freedom Fighters

## ARMS AND THE MAN

The arrest of several Congress leaders during the Quit India movement had weakened the Indian freedom struggle considerably. However, one man provided a much-needed impetus at this time—**Subhas Chandra Bose**. He escaped from his house in Kolkata where he had been kept under British surveillance and travelled abroad to gather the support of Indians living there in order to overthrow the British from India. In 1943, he formed the Azad Hind Fauj or the Indian National Army (INA) in Singapore. With Japanese assistance, the INA headed to India and freed the Andaman and Nicobar islands. Then it moved to Kohima in the North-East and Bose was made the commander-in-chief of the INA on Indian soil. However, with the defeat of Japan in World War II in 1945, the INA lost its support base. Bose was killed in an air crash at Taipei on 18 August 1945 while he was on his way to Tokyo. Even though Subhas Chandra Bose did not live to see India's independence, his revolutionary spirit was carried forward by his powerful words, 'Jai Hind'!

It was Rabindranath Tagore who first addressed Subhas Chandra Bose as 'Netaji' or Respected Leader.

## WOW THINGS ABOUT THE 1857 UPRISING!

• During the Uprising of 1857, freedom fighters like **Nana Sahib**, the **Begum of Awadh** and the **Rani of Jhansi** exchanged plans about strategic meetings through secret messages hidden in chapatis, red lotuses and bits of goats' flesh!

• **Veer Savarkar** wrote a book called *The Indian War of Independence 1857*. It was banned by the British, which meant it could not be printed in India. Thanks to **Madame Bhikaji Cama**, the book was printed in Holland without a cover or a name. It was then cleverly smuggled into India using the cover pages of popular classics like *Don Quixote* and *Oliver Twist*!

## WHAT'S IN A NAME?

Everything, when it came to many of our freedom fighters, who were popularly known by special names that reflected their extraordinary qualities! Here are a few of the popular ones:

**Iron Man of India**: Sardar Vallabhai Patel
**Nightingale of India**: Sarojini Naidu
**Gurudev**: Rabindranath Tagore
**Babasaheb**: B.R. Ambedkar
**Frontier Gandhi**: Khan Abdul Gaffar Khan
**Netaji**: Subhas Chandra Bose
**Punjab Kesari**: Lala Lajpat Rai
**Lokmanya**: Bal Gangadhar Tilak
**Shaheed**: Bhagat Singh
**Mahamana**: Madan Mohan Malaviya

## for Gandhi

**If there is one man synonymous with India's freedom struggle, it is none other than Mohandas Karamchand Gandhi. The epithet 'Mahatma' (Great Soul) was given to him by Rabindranath Tagore and then adopted by the whole country, as he walked his way into people's hearts!**

*Mohandas Karamchand Gandhi as a young boy*

## GLUED TO HIS BOOKS

As a child, Gandhi loved his storybooks. Indian classics, especially tales of the honest King Harishchandra and the noble Shravana, made a great impression on him. Later, in his autobiography, *The Story of My Experiments with Truth*, he recalls enacting the role of King Harishchandra by himself a number of times.

Much later in life, when he ran the Navjivan Press, Gandhi insisted that children's books should be printed in bold typefaces on good paper and be illustrated with sketches. In fact, he considered bad printing an act of himsa or violence! Any surprises why children love the **Father of the Nation** so much?

## WALKING THE TALK

On 12 March 1930, Mahatma Gandhi, accompanied by 78 supporters, began a unique protest march from his Sabarmati Ashram near Ahmedabad. The Mahatma had decided to resume his non-violent Civil Disobedience Movement by dissenting against what many of his supporters felt was a rather unimportant issue—a tax on common salt imposed by the British.

Determined to break the Salt Laws and make his own salt from seawater, Gandhiji set off for the coastal town of Dandi, 390 km away. At 61, the oldest satyagrahi on the Salt March was Gandhiji himself (the youngest was 16!), but he walked with such long strides that the other volunteers could hardly keep up. By the time he reached the coastal town of Dandi in 24 days, thousands of Indians had been inspired to join him in his protest. At sunrise on 6 April 1930, Gandhiji waded into the waters and picked up a pinch of fresh salt, thereby symbolically breaking the law. 'With this, I shake the foundations of the British Empire!' he declared, showing just how salt had everything to do with Swaraj. The pinch of salt was later auctioned to the highest bidder for Rs 1600.

Incidentally, Gandhiji himself had not used salt in his food for six years before the Salt March!

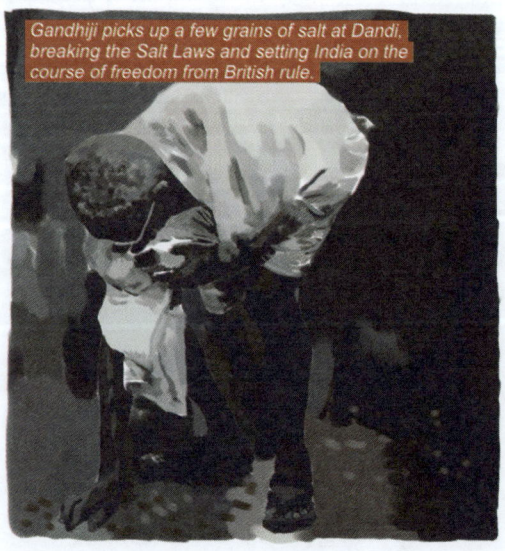

*Gandhiji picks up a few grains of salt at Dandi, breaking the Salt Laws and setting India on the course of freedom from British rule.*

# for Gandhi

## GANDHI GYAN

• Gandhiji's nickname at school was **Moniya** or **Manu**.

• Gandhiji gave up western clothing and adopted the waist-to-knee dhoti or the loincloth in 1921. He carried a set of false teeth in a fold of his loincloth and put them in his mouth only when he wanted to have a meal!

• Gandhi experimented with various diets to see how he could live within modest means and yet remain healthy. So he primarily lived on fruit, goats' milk and olive oil.

• As his popularity as a leader grew, Gandhiji felt that he needed one day of complete silence every week. He decided not to speak on Mondays. These silent Mondays continued right through his life!

• Gandhiji was chosen for the Nobel Peace Prize in 1948. However, he was assassinated before it was conferred upon him. As a mark of respect, the Nobel Committee decided not to award the Peace Prize that year.

• The **Pietermaritzburg** station in South Africa has remained largely unchanged since the time Mahatma Gandhi made that life-changing journey on 7 June 1893 when he was thrown off a train. Several plaques now line the main entrance hall, commemorating the significant event, which shaped Gandhiji's ideas on satyagraha.

• On 15 June 2007, the United Nations General Assembly decided to commemorate Gandhiji's birthday on 2 October as the **International Day of Non-Violence**.

*The world-famous ten-rupee postage stamp depicting Mahatma Gandhi*

## PO GANDHI

A ten-rupee postage stamp depicting Mahatma Gandhi issued by India in 1948 is celebrated for many reasons. A set of 100 of these stamps were overprinted with the word 'service' for official use by the then Governor General of India, C. Rajagopalachari, making it the world's least printed stamp. This 'service' overprinted stamp was sold by David Feldman, a leading philatelist and auctioneer, in 2011, for a staggering US$ 2,05,000, making it the world's most expensive stamp issued in modern times.

The plan to issue a set of stamps depicting Mahatma Gandhi was first made in January 1948. The India Security Press in Nashik was given the job of printing them, but before the stamps were issued, Gandhiji was assassinated. So, the Indian government decided to print these stamps as a memorial using a unique printing method. The services of Helio Courvoisier, a printer from Switzerland, were used, making it India's only postage stamp printed outside the country till date.

The stamps were eventually issued on 15 August 1948, on the first anniversary of India's Independence.

# for Ganga

Rivers are extra-special in India, which is why they have been loved and respected through the ages. Our four sacred rivers—the Ganga, the Brahmaputra, the Narmada and the Kaveri—play a major role in religion, mythology, culture, geography, politics . . . and life itself!

The Ganga flowing near the Gangotri Glacier

## THE GANGA

**Source**: **Gaumukh**, a giant ice-cave on the Gangotri Glacier in Uttarkashi district of Uttarakhand.

**Legend and Lore**: According to Hindu mythology, Ganga was a celestial river goddess who was compelled to come down to earth because of the penance of Sage Bhagiratha. Annoyed, she decided to arrive with a fury that would sweep the earth away. Bhagiratha begged Lord Shiva for help. Shiva caught Ganga as she fell and tied her up in his matted locks. Finally, he let her flow out, but with much less force and power in order to avoid destruction.

### Fab Facts
• The Ganga is 2525 km long and has the most populated river basin in the world. Approximately 400 million people live here!

• The river is home to the endangered Gangetic River Dolphin, which is India's national aquatic animal.

## THE BRAHMAPUTRA

**Source**: The **Jima Yangzong Glacier**, near Mount Kailash, in Tibet, where it is called the Yarlung Tsangpo River.

**Legend and Lore**: Parashurama, an avatar of Lord Vishnu, was forced to behead his mother with an axe at the order of his father. The axe, however, remained stuck to his hand. Parashurama was asked to make a pilgrimage to the Brahmaputra, which was then a sacred lake surrounded by hills. He hacked down the hills, releasing the water of the Brahmaputra into the plains, and was rid of both the axe and his sin.

### Fab Facts
• The 'Brahmaputra' means son of Brahma. It is 2900 km long and is India's only 'male' river.

• It plays the role of both creator and destroyer in India—depositing huge quantities of fertile alluvial soil and also causing disastrous and frequent floods.

The Brahmaputra coursing in serene splendour in Assam

## for Ganga

## THE NARMADA

**Source**: The **Narmada Kund**, a small tank on the Amarkantak Hill in the Anuppur district of eastern Madhya Pradesh.

**Legend and Lore**: There is a story that Lord Shiva was once practising such intense meditation that he began to perspire heavily. His sweat pooled at the Narmada Kund, from where it began to flow as River Narmada! The Narmada is believed to be so sacred that Ganga herself comes and bathes there when she becomes too polluted!

*The 'Narmada' means the giver of pleasure and the river waters Central India.*

**Fab Facts**
• The Narmada is considered to be the dividing line between north and south India. It is our only major river which flows westwards.

• It has 30 dams planned across its length of 1312 km, of which the Sardar Sarovar is the largest and most controversial. Those who support the construction believe that it will ease people's misery in the drought-prone areas of Kutch and Saurashtra. Those who oppose it say it will destroy the environment and displace too many people. The case is being heard in court.

## THE KAVERI

**Source**: **Talakaveri**, in the Brahmagiri hills of Kodagu (Coorg) district in Karnataka.

**Legend and Lore**: Having observed the misery of the people in drought-ridden Kodagu, Kaveri, daughter of the illustrious sage Kavera, prayed that she should be turned into a river. Her wish was granted. But before she could set out on her journey, Sage Agastya asked her to marry him. Kaveri agreed on the condition that he would never leave her alone for long. Agastya agreed, but once got so involved in a debate that he forgot his promise. Kaveri quickly flowed away to become the life-giving river she is today.

**Fab Facts**
• The 765-km-long River Kaveri drops to form the famous Shivanasamudra Falls. Asia's first hydroelectric plant was built here way back in 1902. One of the oldest dams in the world, the Grand Anicut, was built across the Kaveri about 2000 years ago, and is still in use!

• The women of Kodagu wear their sarees back to front. It is said that when Kaveri escaped from Agastya, she rushed towards the women so happily that their saree pleats were pushed all the way to the back!

*The Kaveri forms the Hogenakkal Falls, often called the 'Niagara of India'.*

# for Gods and Goddesses

If we have a population of over a billion people in our country, well, we have a million gods and goddesses in our heavens to watch over us! With each one being worshipped and feted in a different way, the celebration never quite ends in India.

## ONE FOR ALL AND ALL FOR ONE

At a most basic level, Hindus believe that there is one God. Known as the **Brahman**, he is the only reality that exists. He is the supreme universal soul, who has no form or limits. He represents the universe and everything in it. But hey, what about all those gods and goddesses you know of? Well, they simply personify various aspects of this one true God, which is just our way of ensuring that we have countless ways to celebrate divinity based on anything that catches our fancy . . . family traditions, community customs, the seasons and so on.

And wait, there's a divine feminine power too. **Adi Shakti** is the representation of a supreme female power and is often referred to as the Great Divine Mother. How powerful is she? Well, she controls the Brahma-Vishnu-Shiva triumvirate, the devas, the planets and all the heavenly bodies!

The principal deities of the Hindu pantheon are Lord Brahma, Lord Vishnu and Lord Shiva.

## THREE'S COMPANY

**Brahma**, **Shiva** and **Vishnu** are the three important gods in the Hindu pantheon, the three divine aspects of the supreme universal God. Called the trimurti, they symbolize the complete circle of samsara (birth-death-rebirth) in Hinduism: Brahma as creator, Vishnu as preserver or protector and Shiva as destroyer.

Do they do it all on their own? Of course not! The tridevi or three goddesses of Hinduism, who are manifestations of Adi Shakti, lend a helping hand. Brahma is the creator, so he needs knowledge or **Saraswati** to create. Vishnu is the preserver, for which he needs wealth or **Lakshmi**. Finally, Shiva is the destroyer and he needs the power of **Parvati**, **Durga** or **Kali** to wreck and recreate.

NO, NO. WE'RE JUST DRESSED UP FOR THE COSTUME PARTY.

## for Gods and Goddesses

## GOD'S OWN COUNTRY

Our list of gods doesn't end there—we have many more called devas and devis, who are celestial beings representing the supreme universal God. Devas are also called suras and are always at battle with the asuras, their half-brothers, to maintain harmony and peace in the universe.

Much like us, devas and devis have jobs to do. Some of them represent the forces of nature, some have to govern the functioning of the cosmos, and yet others are responsible for upholding moral values. **Indra, Agni, Varuna, Vayu** and **Yama** are important devas as are **Ganesha, Hanuman** and the different avatars of Vishnu, while prominent devis include **Ushas, Aditi** and **Prithvi.** The Rig Veda contains hymns in praise of 33 different devas, who helped defeat asuras and maintain peace in the world.

One of India's best-loved gods, Lord Ganesha

## DESIGNING FOR THE GODS

Who gave the gods their snazzy chariots, cool weapons and awesome palaces? Their very own personal designer, **Vishwakarma!** The presiding deity of engineers, craftsmen and architects, he is believed to be the divine draftsman of the whole universe. The Mahabharata describes him as 'the lord of the arts, executor of a thousand handicrafts, the carpenter of the gods, the most eminent of artisans, the fashioner of all ornaments . . . and a great and immortal god.' Now what wouldn't you do for an all-in-one designer like this one!

## ARE THE GODS VEGGIE . . . OR NOT?

India has more vegetarians than any other country—some 350 million in all. No other country knows how to cook vegetables in so many different ways. In no other country are meat-eaters called 'non-vegetarians'. But how and why did it happen? Here is one theory.

Most Indians did eat meat, some 3500 to 4000 years ago. And ancient stories tell of gods eating meat as well. Animal sacrifice was common, and the sacrificed beast was eaten. It was only 2500 years ago, when Vardhamana Mahavira, who founded Jainism, and Gautama Buddha, who founded Buddhism, arrived on the scene and began to preach about ahimsa (non-violence) that vegetarianism had its first champions. About 300 years after that, Emperor Ashoka became a Buddhist, making vegetarianism even more popular in the country.

# for Handlooms

Cool cottons, soft linen, lustrous silks, heavy brocades, fine wools . . . India offers an array of exquisite handlooms in every colour and weave to drape you!

## GOOD GOD!

The story goes that Sage Markanda wove the first piece of fabric from lotus fibre in order to clothe the gods! With a history that derives from the very heavens, it is no wonder that India's handlooms are renowned in almost every corner of the world today.

Excavations at the Indus Valley Civilization sites prove that people used homespun cotton to weave their garments. Household items like needles of bone, spindles of wood and fragments of woven cotton have been unearthed, which suggest that the history of our handlooms dates back to 5000 years ago.

OUR COOL, MODERN COTTON IS 5000 YEARS OLD? *COOL!*

## DID YOU KNOW?

Next to agriculture, the handloom weaving industry is the largest provider of employment in India.

## HANDLOOM HANDY GUIDE

**Silk** came to India from China, but once it got here, we adapted it and made it our own. The **brocades** of Varanasi are considered the richest of woven silks and use only pure gold or silver threads in the weaving. **Ikat** is the only handloom where the yarn is dyed according to the pattern before it is woven into burnished **patola** and **pochampalli** silks. Kanchipuram is known for creating the most resplendent silks.

Cottons are woven all over India and each area has a distinctive weave, texture or design. **Jamdani** was created as fine cotton fit for royalty. **Himroo** and **Mashru** were woven specially for orthodox Muslims who were not allowed to wear silk. These fabrics have a cotton warp and silk weft, and are woven in such a way that only the cotton touches the skin!

The beauty of many Indian handlooms lies in the fine art of dyeing and printing. **Bandhani** is one of our most colourful tie-dyed fabrics, while textiles from Sanganer and Udaipur have intricate floral designs imprinted on them with wooden blocks.

## WEAVING OUR FREEDOM

Isn't it interesting that the European colonizers came to India for our cottons and indigo and eventually had to leave because of the power of India's very own handspun fabric, **khadi**? Indeed khadi is not just a cloth to us—it symbolizes a powerful movement started by Mahatma Gandhi to boycott foreign goods and win us our freedom.

# for Hill Stations

Have you ever escaped to a cool hill station to beat the summer heat? Well, lucky you, because hill stations are pretty much unique to India!

## HIGH UP IN THE HILLS

Hill stations are picturesque towns that are located at a higher elevation than the plain or valleys near them. The word 'hill station' was mainly used in colonial India for towns founded by European colonizers, who ruled the country before Independence. Hill stations were set up so that foreign officers and their families could escape the scorching summers of the subcontinent.

With nine significant mountain ranges criss-crossing the country, including the **Himalayas**, the **Aravallis**, the **Vindhyas** and the **Eastern** and **Western Ghats**, India, quite naturally, presented many options. Most Indian hill stations are located at an altitude of 3500 to 7500 feet and offer some of the most spectacular landscapes in the world—from snowy peaks and misty mountains to flower-filled meadows and blue lakes.

SIR, THAT ISN'T A TRAIN STATION, IT IS JUST A HILL STATION.

## ONE FOR THE BRITISH

In India, the British primarily set up hill stations all over the country. Did you know that the officers of the British Raj, and the British Army in particular, founded some 50 of the 80-odd hill stations? Guess that's how much they wanted to get away from the heat and dust of the plains! Several hill stations were summer capitals of Indian states till Independence, after which they've remained popular summer retreats.

A little toy train chugging its way up the hills

## TRAIN TO HAPPINESS

Built during the 19th and early 20th century by the British, the **Mountain Railways of India** consists of seven toy trains that run on historic tracks up to various hill stations. Running on a narrow or metre gauge line, these trains wind their way up the hilly terrain, treating passengers to beautiful mountain scenery along the way.

The idea of a mountain railway was first proposed in 1844 by Sir John Lawrence, the Viceroy of India, who suggested 'a phased colonization of the hills'. Work began in 1878 and five masterpieces of engineering were constructed: the Darjeeling-Himalayan Railway, the Nilgiri Mountain Railway, the Kalka-Shimla Railway, the Matheran Hill Railway, and the Kangra Valley Railway. Today, the first three of these railways have been collectively designated a UNESCO World Heritage Site. Climb aboard with a merry song on your lips and chug away to holiday happiness!

## for Hill Stations

# TOP OF THE HILLTOPS
## NORTHERN NIRVANA:
### SHIMLA

Shimla derives its name from Goddess Shyamala Devi, believed to be an avatar of Goddess Kali. A Scottish civil servant named Charles Kennedy built a summer home in Shimla in 1822 and it soon grew to become the summer capital of British India in 1864. After Independence, Shimla became the capital of Punjab and was later made the capital of Himachal Pradesh. When you're there, make sure to munch on juicy apples as you stare at the most scenic line of snow-covered peaks you'll ever see!

Shimla is often called the queen of hill stations.

## SOUTHERN SPLENDOUR:
### KODAIKANAL

Kodaikanal was set up as a sanatorium in 1845 by the American Madurai Mission. Another tale goes that it was founded in 1901 when American missionaries established a school for European children here. Whatever the story, it is the only hill station in India to be established by the Americans. Located on the southern crest of the Palani Hills, it is home to the famed kurinji shrub, whose light purple flowers bloom once every 12 years! Next flowering date: 2018.

## EASTERN EDEN:
### DARJEELING

Established by Arthur Campbell, a surgeon with the East India Company, and Lieutenant Robert Napier in the 1830s, Darjeeling is synonymous with fine teas and five other Ts—teak, toy trains, treks, tourists and Tiger Hill (the highest point in the area). Given to the British as a gift from the king of Sikkim, Darjeeling's charm lies in sipping aromatic tea as you soak in the spectacular sight of the snow-capped Kanchenjunga!

A breathtaking view of the Kanchenjunga from Darjeeling.

## WESTERN WONDER:
### MATHERAN

Perched beautifully on the Western Ghats in Maharashtra, 'Matheran' literally means forest on the forehead of the mountains. Discovered in 1850 by Hugh Poyntz Malet, the district collector of Thane, the hill station still retains the vintage charm of the 18th century because of the absence of tarred roads, and the sound of ponies clip-clopping to transport people across town. Spread over an area of just 8 sq km, Matheran is India's smallest hill station!

# for Himalayas

Ever wondered how the Himalayas got so high? Well, the earth's tectonic plates went crash-smash-boom-bang against each other with such force that its crust folded up into the world's highest mountain range!

## HIGH ON THE HIMALAYAS

It is said that the Himalayas were formed when the Indo-Australian and Eurasian tectonic plates collided with each other. At the time, there was a sea where the mountain range now stands, and this big bang raised the sea floor to form the Himalayas.

The Himalayas border the Indian subcontinent in the north. They stretch for about 2500 km from west to east in a gentle arc and include more than 30 towering peaks rising to heights greater than 24,000 feet. In fact, the ten highest mountains in the world are all in the Himalayas!

### HIGH FIVE

The five highest peaks in the Himalayas are:
**Mount Everest** – 29,029 feet
**K2** – 28,251 feet
**Kanchenjunga** – 28,169 feet
**Lhotse** – 27,940 feet
**Makalu** –27,765 feet

Even though the Himalayas (which means abode of snow in Sanskrit) are about 70 million years old, they are the world's youngest fold mountains!

*The snow-capped peak of the Everest*

## ON THE MOVE

The Himalayas are considered to be geologically alive! The southern front moves about 20 mm a year. So, in ten million years, the Himalayas would have moved approximately 1500 km into Asia!

DO YOU THINK THAT MAKES ME THE FASTEST MOUNTAIN IN THE WORLD?

### IS THERE ANYBODY OUT THERE?

Legend has it that a strange man-like creature called the **Yeti**, or the **Abominable Snowman**, has been seen in the Himalayas. Well, make that man-like or bear-like or orangutan-like or wolf-like or even spirit-like! Does the Yeti really exist? That's a mystery waiting to be solved!

## for Himalayas

## CLIMB EVERY MOUNTAIN

When someone asked the legendary mountaineer George Mallory why he wanted to climb Mount Everest, he said, 'Because it's there!' Well, since it is, here are some fascinating 'first' facts:

### FIRST THINGS FIRST

**First Ascent:** Edmund Hillary and Tenzing Norgay on 29 May 1953
**First Solo Attempt without Oxygen:** Reinhold Messner in 1978
**First Ascent by a Woman:** Junko Tabei in 1975. The first Indian woman to climb it was Bachendri Pal, in 1984.
**Youngest Person to Climb the Everest:** Jordan David Romero (aged 13), in 2010. The youngest Indian girl to climb Mount Everest was Malavath Purna (aged 13 years and 11 months) in 2014. And the youngest Indian boy was Raghav Joneja (aged 15 years and 7 months), in 2013.

## WHY ARE THE HIMALAYAS IMPORTANT TO INDIA?

• The melting snow and glaciers of the Himalayas give rise to many mighty rivers that flow into Pakistan, India and China, including the Indus Basin, the Ganga–Brahmaptura Basin and the Yangtze Basin, which are three of the world's primary river systems. Almost three billion people—that's about half the world's population—depend on the river waters for cultivation, transportation and other means of livelihood.

• The Himalayas form a natural wall between the Indian subcontinent and the Tibet plateau, blocking the icy dry Arctic winds from blowing into South and Central Asia. That's why we don't have severe winters in the country. They also prevent the rain-laden monsoon clouds from the south from crossing over to Tibet. The clouds drop almost all their water south of the Himalayas, making this part of the subcontinent one of the most fertile places in the world.

## ZONING INTO THE HIMALAYAS

The Himalayas are made of three parallel zones or bands:

**THE GREAT HIMALAYAS (OR HIGHER HIMALAYAS)**

**Height:** Over 20,000 feet

**Important ranges:** Zanskar, Ladakh, Kailas

**THE MIDDLE HIMALAYAS (OR THE LESSER HIMALAYAS)**

**Height:** 6000–10,000 feet

**Important ranges:** Nag Tibba, Dhaula Dhar, Pir Panjal

**THE SUB-HIMALAYAS (OR THE OUTER HIMALAYAS)**

**Height:** 3000–4000 feet

**Important range:** Siwaliks (includes the Himalayan foothills, the Indo-Gangetic plains and the Tarai grasslands)

# H

## for Hindustani Music

**Nothing like a great melody to get you humming or a good rhythm to get that foot tapping, isn't it? Well, would you believe that raga (melody) and tala (rhythm) are precisely what distinguish Indian classical music from the other musical forms of the world.**

## NORTHERN NOTES

Hindustani music refers to the North Indian style of classical music that is indigenous to the northern parts of India, Pakistan and Bangladesh and some areas of Nepal and Afghanistan. It traces its origins to Vedic chanting, which dates back to over 3000 years ago, to ancient Persian classical music and to various folk traditions. It is one of the two forms of Indian classical music, the other one being Carnatic music, which is the classical tradition of the south of the country.

Hindustani classical music began flourishing in India with the advent of Islamic rule under the Delhi Sultanate at the end of the 12th century. The most influential musician of the Delhi Sultanate was **Amir Khusrau**, who is often called the father of modern Hindustani classical music.

## MUSIC TO YOUR EARS

Hindustani music is based on the **raga** system. A raga is a melodic scale and the framework to create music is based on a given set of notes with distinctive rhythmic patterns. The rhythmic patterns are set by claps or **talas**, which are essentially divisions in time. The major vocal styles associated with Hindustani classical music are **dhrupad**, **khyal** and **tarana**.

WELL, I DIDN'T THINK MUSIC WAS *THAT* DIFFICULT TO UNDERSTAND...

## OF GURUKULS AND GHARANAS

Gharanas were established in Hindustani music in the 19th century based on the guru-sishya tradition followed at gurukuls. When kings were unable to patronize musicians, the artistes had to move to big cities where they retained their identities by taking the name of the regions they came from. The **Gwalior Gharana** is the oldest gharana and was founded in the 16th century by Nathan Peer Baksh and Nathe Khan.

A Hindustani music concert in progress

# H

## for Howrah Bridge

It bears the weight of approximately 1,00,000 vehicles and 1,50,000 people every day, besides weathering storms and cyclones in the Bay of Bengal! Is this about Superman, the man of steel? No, it is about a bridge of steel—Kolkata's magnificent Howrah Bridge!

## BRIDGE BHASHA

There are four main types of bridges in the world:

**Beam bridges** are beams or slabs supported at either end by natural ground or by a man-made structure. E.g. Lake Pontchartrain Causeway, Louisiana, USA

**Cantilever bridges** are constructed using beams, each supported only at one end. Usually, a tower is built on either side and a beam erected from each tower. The beams meet at the centre to form the bridge. E.g. Howrah Bridge, Kolkata, India

**Arch bridges** have ends that are buried into supports which take the load of the bridge. The arch is a very special shape to give extra strength to the bridge. E.g. Sydney Harbour Bridge, Sydney, Australia

**Suspension bridges** are suspended from steel cables, which hang from high towers. The roadway is supported from one end of the bridge to the other by giant cables. E.g. Golden Gate Bridge, San Francisco, USA

## HOWRAH HANDY GUIDE

• The Howrah Bridge is a suspension type balanced cantilever bridge that stretches across the Hooghly River.

• Commissioned in 1943, the bridge was originally called the New Howrah Bridge, because it links the city of Howrah to Kolkata. On 14 June 1965, it was renamed **Rabindra Setu**, after the Nobel laureate Rabindranath Tagore.

• Howrah Bridge is the busiest cantilever bridge in the world.

• The total length of the bridge is 2313 feet, its height 269 feet and width 71 feet with two footpaths of 15 feet on either side.

• Besides Howrah Bridge, there are three other bridges on the Hooghly— Vidyasagar Setu, Vivekananda Setu and Nivedita Setu.

## HAH AND BAH, HOWRAH!

Can you believe that not a single nut or bolt has been used to build Howrah Bridge? 26,500 tons of steel have been simply fastened by rivets to hold up the structure!

What is one of the important factors causing damage to the bridge? Spitting! An inspection in 2011 revealed that spitting had reduced the thickness of the steel hoods by more than 3 mm since 2007!

## I for Independence

On 15 August 1947, British rule in India came to an end after 163 long years, and India became a free country. Jawaharlal Nehru, our first and longest-serving prime minister, announced to the world that India had finally made her 'Tryst with Destiny'.

## RAJ TO SWARAJ

While several important events spurred India to that eventful midnight hour when we became free, four incidents are regarded as the most significant.

## RISING IN REVOLT

**The Uprising of 1857:** By 1856, almost the whole of India had come under British rule. Everywhere, Indians felt angry and humiliated. On 10 May 1857, in the town of Meerut in Uttar Pradesh, Indian soldiers rebelled against the British officers for forcing them to use cartridges lined with beef and pork fat. It was the beginning of our first organized attempt to revolt against authority. The uprising was crushed ruthlessly by the British government. In August 1858, the East India Company, which had ruled India for a century, was dissolved and Queen Victoria became the ruler of India.

Soldiers rose in protest across the country during The Uprising of 1857.

## INDEPENDENCE OR NOTHING

**The Civil Disobedience Movement of 1929:** In December 1928, Indian leaders gave an ultimatum to the British government to grant India dominion status—that is, the freedom to rule themselves under the supervision of the British king. Gandhiji declared that if India wasn't granted the status within a year, Indians would begin their fight for complete independence. In October 1929, the British viceroy, Lord Irwin, invited Indian leaders to London for a conference to discuss the country's future. However, India's dominion status was not brought up at the meeting and so Gandhiji walked out in protest. On 31 December 1929, at the Congress session in Lahore, Jawaharlal Nehru unfurled the flag of independent India for the first time. On 26 January 1930, the official call for Purna Swaraj or complete independence was made.

## COMMON SALT, UNCOMMON CAUSE

**The Dandi March of 1930:** The Congress realized that just calling for Purna Swaraj wasn't enough. They needed a nationwide movement against the British. Gandhiji was put in charge and he found a cause that would unite every Indian—common salt. To protest against the unfair Salt Tax levied by the British, he set off on a march to the coastal town of Dandi to make his own salt. By the time he got there, thousands of Indians had joined him. The walk eventually shook the foundations of the British empire.

# I

## for Independence

## DO OR DIE

**The Quit India Movement of 1942:** On 8 August 1942, at a session of the All India Congress Committee held at the Gowalia Tank Maidan in Bombay, Mahatma Gandhi demanded that the British leave India immediately, granting us our freedom. His 'Do or Die' call to all Indians galvanized the nation into a non-violent Civil Disobedience Movement. The British realized that India's call for freedom could no longer be ignored.

## MOUNTBATTEN MOVES IN

In February 1947, Prime Minister Clement Attlee announced that the British government would grant full self-governance to India by June 1948. He appointed a new viceroy, Louis Mountbatten, to undertake the job. Lord Mountbatten completed his task in no time. He arrived in Delhi on 22 March 1947, and India and Pakistan declared independence less than five months later. Mountbatten ensured the speedy passage of the Indian Independence Act 1947 through the British Parliament, and at 11.57 p.m. on 14 August 1947 Pakistan was declared a separate nation. At 12.02 a.m., just after midnight, on 15 August 1947, India became an independent country.

The story goes that Nehru was warned by astrologers about August 14 not being an auspicious date for the birth of the country. That is why he signed on the dotted lines just two minutes after midnight!

I WAS THERE, WHEN INDIA GOT HER *INDEPENDENCE!*

## A COUNTRY IS CUT UP

On 3 June 1947, the Indian National Congress and Muslim League leaders met under the chairmanship of Lord Mountbatten and agreed that India would be partitioned. The northern and predominantly Muslim sections of India would become the nation of Pakistan, while the southern and majority Hindu sections would constitute the Republic of India. The Radcliffe Line was drawn, which demarcated the two countries, cutting several villages in its path into half!

Partition saw the largest migration of people in the history of the world. In the space of a few months, about twelve million Hindus, Muslims and Sikhs moved between the new countries, travelling by bus, car and train, but mostly on foot in great columns called kafilas, which could stretch for dozens of miles. The longest of them is said to have had 4,00,000 people! A million people are believed to have died during Partition due to religious riots.

*Lakhs of people boarded trains from India and Pakistan during the Partition to escape the rioting.*

# I for India Gate and Gateway of India

Two glorious monuments, two impressive gateways . . . that welcome you to two of India's most important cities, Delhi and Mumbai.

## MAGNIFICENT MEMORIAL

Situated in the heart of New Delhi on Rajpath, India Gate commemorates the 90,000 Indian soldiers who lost their lives fighting for the British Army during World War I and the Third Afghan War. Designed by Sir Edwin Lutyens, it was inspired by the Arc de Triomphe in Paris. The 42 m tall monument is made of red and pale sandstone and granite. It was originally known as the All India War Memorial. After Independence, it became the site of the Indian Army's Tomb of the Unknown Soldier.

## GRAND GATEWAY

Situated on the waterfront in the Apollo Bunder area, overlooking the Arabian Sea, the Gateway of India was built to commemorate King George V and Queen Mary's visit to Mumbai in 1911. However, the royal couple only got to see a cardboard model because the construction of the monument began much later in 1915! A 26 m high yellow basalt and concrete arch built in the Indo-Saracenic style, the Gateway was considered the ceremonial entrance to India during the British Raj.

India Gate at New Delhi

Gateway of India at Mumbai

## TERRIFIC TRIVIA

• India Gate is one of the largest war memorials in India. Its foundation stone was laid by the Duke of Connaught in 1921. Ten years later, it was dedicated to the nation by Viceroy Lord Irwin.

• The arch of India Gate houses the **Amar Jawan Jyoti**, which was unveiled on 26 January 1972. The flame burns day and night to remind us of soldiers who died in the Indo-Pakistan War of 1971.

• The names of thousands of soldiers who laid down their lives for their country have been etched on the gate's walls.

## TERRIFIC TRIVIA

• The Gateway has often been called the Taj Mahal of Mumbai.

• It was designed by George Wittet and its foundation stone was laid on 31 March 1911 by the Governor of Bombay, Sir George Sydenham Clarke. The Gateway was opened on 4 December 1924 by the Earl of Reading.

• The First Battalion of the **Somerset Light Infantry**, which was the last of the British troops to leave India after Independence, passed through the Gateway in February 1948. It signalled the end of British rule.

# I

## for Indus Valley Civilization

The discovery of the Indus Valley Civilization sites pushed India's history back by 2000 years to 2600 BCE, making our country home to the biggest of the ancient civilizations!

Ruins of the ancient city of Mohenjodaro

## WHO UNEARTHED THE INDUS VALLEY SITES?

Sometime in the 1850s, a railway line was being built between Lahore and Karachi in Pakistan. In the course of the digging, the workmen stumbled upon a number of bricks in very good condition. Some of these bricks were used to lay the tracks. Little did they know that the bricks they were using were almost 4500 years old and that they came from two glorious ancient cities that had flourished around their construction site.

In the 1920s, archaeologist **Sir John Marshall** dug up a mound close to this area and stumbled upon the cities of Harappa and Mohenjodaro buried underground. Since both cities were close to River Indus, he named the civilization that flourished here the Indus Valley Civilization.

## THE BIGGEST AND THE BEST PLANNED

The Indus Valley Civilization spread over an area of 1.25 million km across modern-day India, Pakistan and Afghanistan. It was first believed that Harappa and Mohenjodaro were the only two great cities here, but some 1400 towns and cities have been excavated since then. At its peak, about five million people probably lived in these settlements.

They were the world's first planned cities, all shaped like parallelograms and with broad roads running through them. Every city had a downtown and a residential area, usually on two different levels. The houses were solidly built of baked brick and stone. After all, they actually managed to survive 4000 years! Every house had a toilet and a good drainage system—something we still haven't been able to achieve in our modern cities!

Structures at Harappa reveal a remarkable level of town planning.

# I
## for Indus Valley Civilization

## ISN'T THAT AMAZING?

• In 2001, archaeologists excavating at Mehrgarh, an Indus Valley city, found eleven drilled molar crowns believed to belong to nine adults who were unearthed from a Neolithic graveyard. The discovery pointed to the fact that the world's first dentist, who was accomplished in drilling teeth, came from here!

• A small curved shell excavated at Mohenjodaro is believed to be the world's first button. It was possibly used as an ornament rather than to fasten a garment.

• The world's first artificial dockyard specifically designed to load and unload cargo was unearthed at Lothal, a prominent Indus Valley city.

• The people of the Indus Valley were among the first to develop a system of uniform weights and measures. They even knew the decimal system.

• They designed and built the world's first bullock cart, which doesn't look very different from our present-day ones.

HEY I SOLVED IT! ALIENS CAME AND TOOK THEM TO ANOTHER PLANET. SIMPLE.

## FABULOUS FINDS

**THE GREAT BATH**: It is one of the best-known structures of the Indus Valley Civilization at Mohenjodaro and is referred to as the 'earliest public water tank of the ancient world'. Guess this is where people went in their spare time and splashed around with their friends!

**THE DANCING GIRL**: A tiny bronze statue of a girl wearing lots of bangles on her arms and with her hair in a plait is considered one of most remarkable finds of the Indus Valley Civilization. Do you think she is proof of the fact that these people loved to party?

**JAZZY JEWELLERY**: Archaeologists have found evidence that the Indus Valley people wore lots of jewellery, especially beads, necklaces, earrings, amulets, bangles and brooches. At Harappa, a man was unearthed from his grave, wearing a necklace of more than 300 soapstone beads!

*The exquisite Dancing Girl of Harappa*

## THE END GAME RIDDLE

How did the Indus Valley Civilization end? Again, we don't really know. The civilization started to disappear by around 1900 BCE. A popular theory is that the Aryan invaders came in from the west and massacred everyone. However this argument has been generally disproved simply because no evidence of weapons, armies or battles have been found. Another theory says a great flood wiped them out. Guess what you can do is put on your thinking caps, because here's a fascinating mystery waiting to be solved!

## I for Information Technology

Say the words 'information technology' in India and surely Bangalore comes to mind. Called the Silicon Valley of India, it was ranked the fourth best global hub of technological innovation in the world by the United Nations!

● ● ● ● ● ● ● ● ● ● ● ● ● ● ● ● ● ● ● ● ●

## INDIA GETS IT RIGHT

Information Technology or IT has been the buzzword in India for at least two decades now. Thanks to IT, we have been declared a knowledge economy, that is, a country which produces wealth and economic benefits for its people by using information.

According to the National Association of Software and Service Companies or NASSCOM, the governing body for software services in India, IT accounted for 1.2 per cent of India's Gross Domestic Product or GDP (the market value of all the goods manufactured and services produced in a country in a given period of time) in 1998 to 7.7 per cent in 2017. Now what does that giant leap really mean for us? Lots of jobs for people who have an education, so make sure you hit those books! The major IT cities in India are Bangalore, Hyderabad, Chennai, Mumbai and Delhi.

The impressive Infosys campus at Electronic City, Bangalore's first software park.

## FROM BOILED BEANS TO SILICON CHIPS

**Bangalore** is often called the Silicon Valley of India because it is the country's leading IT exporter. Why exporter? Because most of the software and services developed here are meant for use in other countries. Bangalore contributes 38 per cent of India's IT exports, and many of India's successful IT companies like Infosys and Wipro are headquartered here. The name Silicon Valley reinforces Bangalore's status as a hub for IT companies in India much like the original Silicon Valley in California, USA.

But did you know that Bangalore was originally called **Benda Kaalooru** or the town of boiled beans? Yes, the story goes that the Hoysala king Veera Ballala was lost in a forest while on a hunting expedition. Tired and hungry, he landed at the hut of an old woman who was cooking a meal of boiled beans for herself. When the king begged for a bite to eat, the old lady generously shared her meal, offering the larger portion to her guest. In honour of his kind hostess, the king named the town Benda Kaalooru, which eventually got shortened to **Bengaluru**!

## BITS AND BYTES

Can the name of a city be used as a verb? Yes, if that city happens to be Bangalore! When a person, especially an American, says he has been **Bangalored**, he means that he has lost his job because his company (in order to cut costs) has moved its operations to a city in India—not necessarily Bangalore!

# J for Jallianwalla Bagh

On 13 April 1919, some 1000 Indians were shot dead in cold blood by British soldiers in a beautiful walled garden in Amritsar. The shameful incident sent shock waves through India and turned our cry for freedom into a deafening roar.

## JAIL WITHOUT FAIL

During the First World War, India helped Britain by sending troops to battle. In return, however, the British did not keep the promises they had made to the Indian people. This led to fierce protests in many parts of the country, especially Punjab and Bengal. To restore order, the British imposed the Rowlatt Act in March 1919. It was an unfair legislation by which any Indian could be jailed without checking if he was guilty or not. India was furious, and Punjab especially so. On 13 April 1919, the British government enforced martial law in Punjab.

### PAST AND PRESENT

• It is believed that **Bhagat Singh**, who was 11 years old at the time of the massacre, became a revolutionary after the incident. **Motilal Nehru** gave up his legal practice to fight for India's freedom and **Rabindranath Tagore** renounced his knighthood in protest.

• When you visit Amritsar, make sure to pay your respects inside the faithfully preserved garden, where you can still see bullet holes in the walls and the tragic **Martyrs' Well**, from which over a 100 bodies were pulled out.

## PELL-MELL IN THE PARK

On the same day that martial law was declared, around 15,000 people had gathered for a public meeting at 4.30 p.m. at Jallianwalla Bagh. Most of them had no idea about the new law and no one was armed. At 5.30 p.m., **Brigadier General Reginald Dyer**, a British army officer, marched into the park with 90 armed soldiers. The soldiers formed a semicircle, blocking the main exit of the park. Then, without a word of warning, Dyer ordered his men to fire. The soldiers did not stop for ten whole minutes, until all their 1650 rounds of ammunition were finished.

Men, women and children ran in panic. Many were shot dead as they tried to climb the walls, and hundreds died in the stampede. Several jumped into a well to escape the bullets and drowned. By 5.45 p.m. when the firing ended, over a 1000 people were dead and many wounded. Dyer simply drove away after his mission was accomplished.

The Jallianwala Bagh incident galvanized the nation into action. Protests broke out across India. Dyer was labelled 'the butcher of Amritsar' and dismissed from the army.

*A monument enclosing the fateful well into which people jumped to escape the bullets fired by the soldiers.*

# for Jama Masjid

Decorated domes, towering minarets, grand entranceways and exquisite architecture come together to form Islam's holiest place of worship and spiritual centre ... the mosque.

## MOSQUE OF THE WORLD

The **Masjid-i-Jahan Numa** was built by the Mughal Emperor Shah Jahan in 1656 CE. Located in Old Delhi in the colourful Chandni Chowk area, it is India's largest and best-known mosque. It derives the name that it is popularly known by, **Jama Masjid**, from the jummah or the Friday noon prayers of the Muslims. It houses several important relics, including an antique copy of the Quran written on deer skin. The mosque is surrounded by bustling bazaars, so once you're done nourishing your soul, treat your stomach to yummy kebabs and tandoori delights in all shapes, sizes and spice quotients!

The 'Masjid-i-Jahan Numa' or the World-Reflecting Mosque in Old Delhi

The Cheraman Juma Masjid

## OLD IS GOLD

The **Cheraman Juma Masjid**, located in Kodungalloor, Kerala, is considered to be India's first mosque. It was built in 629 CE by Malik Ibn Dinar, who is said to be the first follower of the Prophet to have set foot in India. The story goes that King Cheraman Perumal of Kodungalloor undertook a journey to Mecca, where he embraced Islam. On his way back to India, he fell terribly ill, and while on his deathbed, he asked his Arab companion Malik Ibn Dinar to go to his kingdom and spread the message of Islam. A group of Arabs led by Malik Ibn Dinar came to Kodungalloor, built a masjid here and named it after King Cheraman. It is believed that the Mappila Muslims of Kerala owe their origins to Malik Ibn Dinar!

REMEMBER GIRLS, WHERE THERE IS A WILL, THERE ARE *MANY* WAYS.

## FLOWER POWER

Even if it is not India's largest or grandest mosque, the **Moti Masjid** of Bhopal is famous because it is one of the few mosques in history that was built by a woman. Sikandar Jahan Begum, its builder, was the ruler of Bhopal between 1844 and 1868. She was a trendsetter in many ways. She never observed purdah, was trained in the martial arts and fought many battles during her reign. The architecture of the Moti Masjid or Pearl Mosque that she constructed is typical of its time with tall brick-red minarets and exquisite marble work.

## for Jama Masjid

The Haji Ali Dargah was constructed in memory of Sayyed Peer Haji Ali Shah Bukhari, a wealthy Muslim merchant.

## CONTROVERSY'S CHILD

The **Babri Masjid** was a mosque in Ayodhya, a city in Uttar Pradesh. It was constructed in 1527 CE by Babur, the first Mughal emperor of India, and was named after him. On 6 December 1992, the mosque was destroyed when a political rally morphed into a mob of some 1,50,000 people. They claimed that the site of the mosque was the former location of a Rama temple since Ayodhya was thought to be his birthplace. India was rocked by communal riots after the destruction of the mosque.

## DARGAHS FOR DEVOTEES

A well-known mosque because of its unique location in the middle of the sea in Mumbai, the **Haji Ali Dargah** is a wonderful example of Indo-Islamic architecture. Constructed in 1431 CE in memory of a wealthy Muslim merchant, Sayyed Peer Haji Ali Shah Bukhari, who gave up all his worldly possessions before making a pilgrimage to Mecca, the mosque welcomes people from all communities. The islet on which it is located is connected to the mainland by a kilometre-long causeway, which gets flooded in high tide, making the mosque accessible only during low tide!

A shrine that gave an emperor his heir and a nation its new king, the powerful, wish-granting dargah of **Salim Chisti** is the place that childless couples throng even to this day in the hope of being blessed with an offspring. It is said that Emperor Akbar walked to this dargah in Fatehpur Sikri to pray for a child. Soon after, his favourite queen Jodha Bai gave birth to a son, whom they named Salim (later known as Jahangir) after the Sufi saint. After the saint's passing, Akbar constructed a beautiful marble mausoleum in his memory.

The **Ajmer Sharif** or the Holy Dargah is a shrine dedicated to Khwaja Moinuddin Chisti, a Sufi saint who did a lot for the welfare of the underprivileged people of Ajmer. Often called the 'Mecca of South Asia', the mosque is an outstanding example of communal harmony. Its silver gates are open to everyone irrespective of religion, caste or social status. Two huge cauldrons of kheer are cooked at the mosque every day to feed devotees. Do you know since when these vessels have been in use? From the time of emperors Akbar and Jahangir, who had donated a cauldron each to the dargah!

SINCE THE TIME OF *AKBAR*? SOMEONE'S BEEN WASHING THEM, RIGHT?

# for Jawaharlal Nehru

A barrister, a nationalist leader, a prolific writer, a statesman, Jawaharlal Nehru wore many hats before he became independent India's first prime minister. He was also the architect who shaped modern India.

The children's favourite uncle, Chacha Nehru

## MATHS IS A NO-NO!

When he was 16, Jawaharlal Nehru's father, Motilal Nehru, sent him to England to study for the Indian Civil Service exams. He enrolled for a course in natural sciences at Trinity College, Cambridge University. As part of this course, Nehru had to study physics, chemistry and mathematics. Nothing unusual there, except that maths was Nehru's big bugbear! So, on request, he was allowed to swap mathematics for botany! Do you think he took the easy way out? No way. Not only did he get an honours degree in natural sciences, but also received a degree in law at the Inner Temple in London before returning home to India.

## FROM LAWYER TO LEADER

Nehru first met Gandhiji at the annual meeting of the Indian National Congress at Lucknow in 1916 and was deeply influenced by his ideas. In 1919, while travelling on the upper berth of a train, Nehru is believed to have overheard a callous conversation between some British officers, one of whom introduced himself as General Dyer and spoke triumphantly about carrying out the massacre at Jallianwalla Bagh. This incident changed Nehru's life forever. He gave up his legal practice to fight against the British in India.

## EDUCATION FOR ALL

Nehru firmly believed that India's future was in the hands of her children and that every single one of them must have access to an excellent education. He oversaw the setting up of many institutions of higher learning, including the All India Institute of Medical Sciences, the Indian Institutes of Technology, the Indian Institutes of Management and the National Institutes of Technology. Not just that, he also guaranteed free and compulsory primary education for all the children of India in the Five Year Plans. That's why children call him **Chacha Nehru** to this day, and his birthday on 14 November is celebrated as Children's Day in India.

IT WAS A YES FOR *DR NO*, BUT A NO FOR *NEHRU*.

## NATTY NEHRU

A hip-length tailored coat with a mandarin collar modelled on the Indian sherwani is a fashion statement today. Can you guess who inspired this creation? Jawaharlal Nehru, of course, and what we're describing here is the famous **Nehru jacket**! By the way, Nehru himself never wore the jacket. However, several popular villains from the early James Bond films appeared in Nehru jackets!

# for J.R.D. Tata

**Credited with building one of India's biggest industrial houses and putting Indian business on the world map long before information technology did, Jehangir Ratanji Dadabhoy Tata, or JRD as he was popularly known, was the king of Indian enterprise!**

## TATA, THE TYCOON

JRD joined Tata & Sons as an unpaid apprentice in 1925. In 1938, when he was just 34, he was elected chairman of the company. He was the youngest member on the board then. Over the next 50 years, he expanded the existing businesses in steel, power and hospitality and diversified into chemicals, automobiles, IT and financial services. In 1938, when JRD took over, the group included 14 companies with sales of 280 crore rupees. In 1991, when he stepped down as chairman, the group comprised 50 companies with sales of 15,000 crore rupees, making it India's biggest business group.

How did JRD achieve all this? By maintaining the highest ethical standards and refusing to pay a single bribe! And by making his workers feel valued. He created the eight-hour workday for employees of Tata Steel, when factories in the West worked 10-12 hour shifts. He also instituted a new practice where a worker was considered to be 'at work' from the moment he left home for work till he got back home from work, which means the company looked after him right through!

NOW, ALL WE NEED IS A PRACTICE WHERE WE CAN REMAIN AT HOME AND BE CONSIDERED 'AT WORK'.

## UP, UP AND AWAY!

Flying was JRD's passion. On 10 February 1929, he became the first Indian to pass the pilot's examination. He had a No.1 stamped on his flying licence because it was the first one to be issued in India! In 1932, he set up Tata Air Mail, a courier service connecting Karachi, Ahmedabad, Bombay and Madras. Some years later, he re-branded his airmail service as Tata Airlines, making it India's first domestic carrier. In 1946, JRD changed the company's name to **Air India**, which remains one of our national airlines to date.

*J.R.D. Tata was known as the father of Indian civil aviation and was awarded the Bharat Ratna in 1992.*

## FLYING HIGH

In 1930, JRD competed in the Aga Khan trophy in which he was flying solo from India to England. He took off from Karachi and was bound for London. En route, when he stopped at Aboukir Bay in Egypt, he found that another contender, **Aspy Engineer**, was stranded because his spark plug was faulty. JRD sportingly lent him his spare one and both of them continued on their flights. Aspy beat JRD by a couple of hours in the contest! Aspy Engineer eventually went on to become the second chief of the Indian Air Force.

## for Kalidasa

**He has been called the Shakespeare of the East, and his writings have been translated into several languages across the world. Meet the greatest Indian poet and playwright of all time—Kalidasa!**

## DULL TO DAZZLING

Not much is known about Kalidasa's life, except that he lived during the fourth or fifth century CE, and wrote brilliant poems and plays in Sanskrit, based on the Hindu Puranas. But he was no superstar to begin with. In fact, he was actually considered a dunce! Kaildasa's life took a curious turn when a crafty minister tricked the princess of the land into marrying him.

The princess soon grew ashamed of the dim-witted Kalidasa and tried to humiliate him. Kalidasa, who was a great devotee of Kali, prayed to the goddess for help. She answered his prayers and granted him the boon of wit and wisdom. He began writing plays and poems that sparkled with beautiful descriptions of nature. Soon he became the most renowned among the Nine Gems at the court of King Vikramaditya of Ujjain.

### KALIDAS SAMMAN

The Kalidas Samman is a very prestigious award named after the great poet. It is presented every year by the Government of Madhya Pradesh for outstanding achievement in classical music, dance and theatre.

## KALIDASA'S FAMOUS FIVE

Kalidasa's best-known works are *Kumarasambhava*, *Ritusamhara* (the first book to be printed in Sanskrit), *Meghaduta*, and *Raghuvamsa*. However, *Abhijnanasakuntalam* (Shakuntala Recognized) is considered his masterpiece.

It tells the story of King Dushyanta and the lovely Shakuntala, whom he meets and marries while on a hunting expedition. Later, Dushyanta has to return to his palace, leaving her behind. When he is away, Shakuntala loses the ring that he had gifted her. The curse of the sage Durvasa makes Dushyanta forget his beloved wife completely, till the ring is found, after which they are reunited and live happily ever after.

*Artist Raja Ravi Varma's painting of a scene from Kalidasa's play, Abhijnanasakuntalam.*

## K

### for Kanyakumari

**When an occasion such as Independence Day is observed across the country, people often say it is celebrated from Kashmir to Kanyakumari. Right? So what's special about these places?**

## LEGEND AND LORE

Kanyakumari gets its name from Goddess Kanyakumari who performed penance there, and killed the wicked demon king Bana. There are many other myths about this place as well. During Rama's war with Ravana in Lanka, Rama's brother Lakshmana was severely wounded. To save him, Hanuman went to the Himalayas and chipped off a whole mountain peak where the life-saving sanjeevani herb grew. When he was carrying it back to Lanka, a chunk of the mountain fell near Kanyakumari, and rare medicinal plants still grow there.

Kanyakumari was ruled by powerful dynasties, like the Cholas, Cheras, Pandyas and Nayaks, as well as the Tranvancore kings. It became a part of the Indian Union after Independence.

## NORTH, SOUTH, EAST AND WEST

The northernmost point of the country, the **Siachen Glacier**, is in the state of Jammu and Kashmir. And **Kanyakumari** (or Cape Comorin) in Tamil Nadu is at the southernmost tip of the Indian mainland, where the waters of the Arabian Sea, the Bay of Bengal and the Indian Ocean meet. And when there is a full moon, you can see the sun set and the moon rise at the same time, over the ocean! The southernmost point of India, however, is **Indira Point** in the Andaman and Nicobar Islands.

The easternmost tip of the country is **Kibithu**, in Arunachal Pradesh; and the last inhabited place in the extreme west is **Guhar Moti** in Kutch, Gujarat.

### LANDMARKS OF KANYAKUMARI

• Memorial to Mahatma Gandhi

• Vivekananda Rock Memorial, built where Swami Vivekananda once sat in meditation for three continuous days and nights

• A 41 m tall figure of the Tamil saint-poet, Thiruvalluvar, which is one of Asia's biggest statues

*The Vivekananda Rock Memorial at Kanyakumari is both a sacred monument and a popular tourist attraction.*

# for Kashmir

Amidst the soaring Himalayas and their forested foothills is a place so beautiful that Mughal Emperor Jahangir called it Paradise on Earth. It is Kashmir, of course!

## WHAT'S IN A NAME?

Geologists believe that Kashmir was once a huge lake. According to legend, Sage Kashyapa drained it by creating a gap in the hills, through the power of his prayers. So it came to be called Kashyapamira and that later became Kashmir. Another belief is that Kashmir got its name from the Khasis who lived there over 2500 years ago.

MONEY CAN MOVE MOUNTAINS!

## WATER, WATER, EVERYWHERE!

Centuries ago, the River Vitasta (now called the Jhelum) was blocked by silt and rocks. So Kashmir was flooded time and again, causing severe famine. A wise man called Suya thought of two smart plans to tackle this recurring crisis. First, he threw silver and gold coins into the water, wherever the river was clogged. Immediately, hordes of people jumped into the water and cleared the silt and boulders to search for the coins! Suya then dug canals to carry some of the water away from the river to irrigate vast areas. That way, more land was cultivated and the region flourished.

## FACT FILE

Kashmir is the northernmost geographical region of our country. Earlier, only the valley between the Great Himalayas and the Pir Panjal range was called Kashmir. Presently, the territory is part of the larger region of Kashmir, which has been the subject of dispute between India, Pakistan and China since 1947. A legislation passed by the Parliament in 2019 reorganised the state of Jammu and Kashmir into two union territories: Jammu and Kashmir and Ladakh.

**AREA:** 2,22,236 sq km

**CAPITAL OF J & K:** Srinagar (summer capital), Jammu (winter capital)

**MAIN OCCUPATIONS:** Carpet weaving, wood carving, handicrafts, tourism and agriculture

**FAMOUS FOR:** Its spectacular scenery, which draws millions of tourists from all over the world

**Hangul**, an endangered species of deer found only in Kashmir

**Saffron**, the divinely fragrant but very expensive spice

**Pashmina shawls** made from the fine wool of Pashmina goats

**Wazwan** or the ultimate feast of 36 mouth-watering dishes

## for Kashmir

*Shikaras on the Dal Lake bring you groceries, fruits and vegetables, and even take you for a spin.*

## MUST-SEE SPOTS

• The spectacular **Dal Lake** is a favourite with visitors. They love to stay on the houseboats there and buy the things that attract them like flowers, vegetables and handicrafts from the vendors in shikaras (small wooden boats) that glide past.

• Those who want to play golf on top of the world, or go skiing, opt for **Gulmarg**.

• The sacred **Amarnath Temple**, of course, is a must for pilgrims.

## THE KASHMIR CONFLICT

With India's Independence from British rule, in 1947, came the Partition of the country into India and Pakistan. Both countries claimed Kashmir and fought over it, although its ruler, Maharaja Hari Singh, had signed an agreement that made Kashmir a part of India. The conflict came to an end through the efforts of the United Nations (UN), leaving portions of Kashmir under the control of each country. But relations between India and Pakistan steadily worsened.

Clashes over Kashmir again resumed, and the Indo-Pak War in 1965 saw the biggest tank battle since World War II. During the Siachen Conflict in 1984, India wrested control of the Siachen Glacier, the highest and most dangerous battleground in the world and the northernmost point of our nation.

Later, in the bitter chill of February 1999, Pakistani troops and Kashmiri militants occupied Indian territory in Kargil. Their plan was to cut off all links between the Kashmir Valley and Ladakh. However, the Indian army put up a fierce fight and the Pakistanis were pushed back. But the Indo-Pak border remains the scene of discord and conflict to date.

*'Gulmarg' means meadow of flowers. It is one of India's most scenic hill stations.*

# for Koh-i-Noor

**It is one of the biggest diamonds in the world, and so bright that it is called Koh-i-Noor, which means mountain of light in Persian. But is it cursed?**

*The coronation crown of Queen Alexandra with the Koh-i-Noor set in the jewelled cross*

## STRANGE STORIES

There are many strange stories about the famed Koh-i-Noor diamond. It is said to have been mined in the 13th century in Kollur, and the Kakatiya rulers there converted it into one of the eyes of their family deity. When Sultan Ghiyas-ud-din Tughlaq swooped down from Delhi and defeated the Kakatiyas, the Koh-i-Noor was part of the enormous loot he carted back with him. The diamond then passed from dynasty to dynasty—Rajput, Mughal, Persian, Afghan, Sikh and British—leaving a trail of blood and betrayal.

What is the Koh-i-Noor worth? Enough 'to feed the whole world for two-and-a-half days', was what Mughal Emperor Babar wrote in his book, *Baburnama*.

## IS THE KOH-I-NOOR CURSED?

Rulers who came into possession of the diamond lost their heads, or their thrones, or faced severe hardships. Humayun, for instance, led a very troubled life, filled with misfortune. The diamond passed on to Sher Shah Suri, who defeated Humayun, but later a canon exploded and killed him. Mughal Emperor Shah Jahan adorned his famous Peacock Throne with the Koh-i-Noor . . . and he was mercilessly dethroned and imprisoned by his son Aurangzeb.

The Persian king Nader Shah, who invaded India and took away the Koh-i-Noor along with the Peacock Throne, was later assassinated. His successors came to a sticky end and his empire crumbled.

EAT THE KOHINOOR?

TOO HARD!

## THE CONTROVERSY

The Koh-i-Noor left India in 1850. If you want to see it, visit the Tower of London, for it is kept there now as part of the **Crown Jewels** belonging to the Queen of England. The Government of India has asked for the return of the diamond, while Pakistan and Iran claim it too!

WHO WOULD'VE THOUGHT THAT A STONE THIS SIZE CAN CAUSE INTERNATIONAL TROUBLE!

## for Kumbh Mela

**Where would you find crowds of people—young and old, rich and poor—singing, dancing, praying and mingling together regardless of caste or creed? At the various melas celebrated all over the country, for sure!**

●●●●●●●●●●●●●●●●●●●●●●●●●

## THE GREATEST SHOW ON EARTH

'Kumbh' means pot or pitcher and 'mela' means fair. And India's Kumbh Mela is by far the world's biggest religious gathering. Want to know why?

Hindus believe that the devas (gods) and asuras (demons) jointly churned the cosmic ocean to obtain amrita (the nectar of immortality). After much huffing and puffing, the pot (kumbh) of nectar popped up, and the gods and demons fought fiercely over it. In the free-for-all, a few drops of nectar fell to earth in four places—Prayag (Allahabad) at the confluence of the rivers Ganga, Yamuna and the mythological Sarasvati, Haridwar on the Ganga, Nashik on the Godavari, and Ujjain on the Shipra. So for centuries, the Kumbh Mela has been held, by rotation, in these four places. A ritual bath in these holy rivers during the Kumbh Mela is said to wash away all sins.

I AM GOING THERE TO SEE IF I CAN WASH AWAY MY TEST RESULTS.

## KUMBH KALEIDOSCOPE

An estimated 240 million people participated in the Kumbh Mela of 2019, held in Prayagraj (formerly Allahabad). They came by car, bus, train, plane or on foot—saints and ash-covered sadhus with matted hair and tridents, the rich and the famous, and hordes of ordinary folks—for a dip in the sacred waters there. In fact, the crowds were so huge that they were visible from satellites in space.

A colossal township was built just for the mela, with tents, fire stations, police stations, post offices and shops for the convenience of visitors. The Uttar Pradesh government is believed to have spent Rs 4236 crore on upgradation of facilities, including installing a record-breaking number of 1.2 lakh eco-friendly toilets! Given the scale and grandeur of the mela, it is no wonder that the Kumbh has been accorded the status of 'Intangible Cultural Heritage of Humanity' by UNESCO.

*Pilgrims at the Kumbh Mela taking a dip in the sacred waters to wash away their sins.*

## for Kumbh Mela

## DIP, DIP, DIP

The **Gangasagar Mela** in West Bengal is the second largest fair after the Kumbh Mela. Lakhs of pilgrims chant prayers, sing songs, and take a dip in the holy waters where River Ganga meets the sea, for they believe that it will wash away their sins. As in most melas, there is an explosion of vibrant colours, sights and sounds, shops selling handicrafts and souvenirs, not to mention the presence of magicians and jugglers.

## TWO-IN-ONE SUPERSTAR

The **Pushkar Mela** in Rajasthan blends both religion and trade. There, devotees first bathe in the Pushkar Lake, which is considered sacred. Then, they worship at the holy Brahma temple, which is believed to be the world's only shrine to Lord Brahma.

The Pushkar Mela is also the world's largest camel fair. So the huge crowds soon set out for some fun, festivities and the business of buying and selling camels and horses too. Some might join in the singing and dancing, watch daring child acrobats, play a game of cricket, or try their luck in the longest moustache competition or, maybe, the turban tying one. Those who would rather spend time with the camels opt for camel racing or camel milking, and there's even a prize for the best camel haircut!

## ENTER THE ELEPHANTS

Elephants being washed and taken to the Haathi Bazaar

The **Sonepur Mela** in Bihar, at the confluence of the Ganga and the Gandak, is one of Asia's biggest cattle fairs. But a large number of elephants are also sold here, in the imposing Haathi Bazaar! Those who visit the fair also worship at the Hariharnath temple, which is said to have been built by Lord Rama himself. In earlier times, the Sonepur Mela was so famous that traders from as far away as Central Asia travelled all the way there to buy and sell their wares.

# for Ladakh

**If you find gompas (Buddhist monasteries) perched on dizzying cliffs, and thukpa (noodle soup), isskyu (pasta and root vegetables) and ngampe (roasted barley flour) on the menu, you're in Ladakh!**

## PEAKS AND PASSES

The union territory of Ladakh is known as Little Tibet because it has been hugely influenced by the Tibetan way of life and culture. The word 'Ladakh' means the land of high passes, and some of the most important passes that connect Ladakh with the rest of the country are the Rohtang Pass, Zoji La and Khardung La.

Ladakh is enveloped by the towering Himalayas and Karakoram Range and criss-crossed by picturesque valleys through which flow many rivers, such as the Indus, Zanskar, Doda, Nubra and Tsarap. Yet, much of Ladakh is an icy cold desert!

## SONG AND DANCE

The people of Ladakh are mostly Buddhists, and religious chanting and dancing are a part of their culture. The colossal 17th century Hemis gompa, for instance, is famous not only for having the longest thangka (Buddhist religious painting) in the world, but also for its colourful dance festival. That's when masked monks dance to the clashing of cymbals and the rumble of drums, enacting the battle between good and evil, with the good triumphing in the end.

*In earlier times, Leh was at the crossroads of important trade routes that linked it with Central Asia and China.*

## HIGHEST OF THE HIGH!

• The highest airport in India is in **Leh**, the capital of Ladakh.

• The **Siachen Glacier** in the north of Ladakh is the most elevated battleground in the whole world.

• Ladakh is one of the highest and coldest inhabited areas on earth.

• The wheat and barley fields there, at **Korzok**, are the highest cultivated fields in all of India.

• Some of the highest motorable roads in the world are in Ladakh.

• Ladakh teems with wildlife, including rare endangered species that live at high altitudes, such as the **snow leopard** and the **Eurasian lynx**.

## for Lakes

India is dotted with lakes, both natural and man-made, in all shapes, sizes and colours—from jade green to sky blue to muddy brown. They are everywhere—in the folds of mountains, spanning flower-strewn valleys, and even in our crowded, polluted cities.

### SAVE OUR LAKES!

So what's the big deal about lakes? They are important because they provide water for drinking, washing and agriculture. They also support a huge variety of animals, birds and plants. Many wildlife sanctuaries are near lakes. Sadly, nowadays, sewage and waste are often dumped in lakes, poisoning the water and harming those that depend on them.

UMMM... IS THAT A SPELLING MISTAKE OR ARE YOU REALLY PLANNING TO DO IT?

SHAVE OUR LAKES

## THE SPECIAL SEVEN

## HEAVENLY HIGHS

Way up in the Himalayas, some 5500 metres above sea level is India's highest lake. It is **Cholamu Lake** in Sikkim, just 5 km from the country's border with China. **Lake Gurudongmar**, which comes a close second, is also in Sikkim, and is named after Guru Padmasambhava (also known as Guru Dongmar). In winter, the entire lake freezes over, except for a small patch, which pilgrims believe was blessed by the guru.

Pushkar Lake is said to be so holy that Pushkar is called the king of pilgrim centres.

## SACRED AND SECULAR

**Pushkar Lake** in Rajasthan is considered sacred by Hindus. According to mythology, when Brahma the Creator dropped a lotus, it turned into Pushkar Lake. There are innumerable temples around the lake, including one of the few Brahma temples in the world. Every year, the largest camel fair in Asia is held at Pushkar. Hordes of people who attend the fair take a dip in the lake, believing it will wash away their sins.

## THE WONDERS OF WULLAR

The **Dal Lake** might be more famous, with its fancy houseboats and the exquisite backdrop of the Mughal gardens. But **Wullar Lake**, which is also in the state of Jammu and Kashmir, is extra-special because it is the biggest freshwater lake in India. It is surrounded by jagged, snow-clad mountains, and teems with fish and birds such as the monal and the Himalayan golden eagle. Wullar figures on the list of Ramsar Sites, which means it is one of the 'wetlands of international importance'.

# L for Lakes

## THE LONGEST ONE

The **Vembanad Lake** in Kerala is the largest saltwater lake in the state and the longest lake in India. Moreover, the lengthiest railway bridge in the country, the Vembanad Rail Bridge, stretches across it. The lake fizzes with action and colour during Onam (Kerala's New Year), when the exciting Snake Boat Race is held, and long boats manned by 100 oarsmen compete against one another. Flocks of migratory birds nest by the lake, at the Kumarakom Bird Sanctuary.

During the Snake Boat Race at the Vembanad Lake, men row to the rhythm of the rousing songs they sing, and the competition is fierce.

The Lonar Lake, which was carved out by a falling meteorite

## AWESOME ACTION FROM OUTER SPACE

Do you know where you'll find the only lake in India carved by a crashing meteorite? Head for **Lonar** in Maharashtra, for that's where a meteorite smashed into the earth, over 50,000 years ago. It created a colossal crater with a saltwater and soda lake, at the bottom!

## THE CHARMS OF CHILKA

Orissa's **Chilka Lake** is the largest saltwater lake in the country. Thousands of migratory birds like cranes, flamingos and geese come from Russia, Iran and Mongolia, to nest there. The lake also supports many species of birds and animals (including endangered ones like dolphins) that it is one of the hotspots of biodiversity on the Indian subcontinent.

## THE LAKE OF FLOATING ISLANDS

**Loktak Lake** in Manipur is the largest freshwater lake in the North-East and the country's only 'floating lake', so called because of its phumdis or thick, large, floating clumps of weeds covered with soil. Fishermen who make a living from the fish there even build their houses on the phumdis! The lake also provides water for drinking, irrigation and power.

# L for Languages

## IN THE BEGINNING . . .

The earliest script discovered in the Indian subcontinent goes way back to the Indus Valley Civilization, about 5000 years ago. It is in the form of pictograms (a pictogram is a picture that represents something), which were carved on seals and pottery. What do they say? No one has decoded this writing and solved the puzzle yet!

The earliest inscriptions in India that have been cracked are the edicts of the Mauryan Emperor Ashoka, carved on rocks and pillars, in the third century BCE. Many of these are in an ancient language called **Brahmi**. Some scholars feel its alphabet was based on Aramaic, which developed in Mesopotamia (now a part of Iraq) before 1000 BCE, and spread east because of trade, while others say Brahmi originated here in India.

A pictogram carved on an Indus Valley seal

## LANGUAGES, LANGUAGES!

The innumerable languages of India fall into roughly four groups: **Indo-European**, **Dravidian**, **Austro-Asiatic** and **Sino-Tibetan**. A majority of the languages of India are descended from **Sanskrit**, which, like Latin and Greek, belongs to the Indo-European family. Even our official language, **Hindi**, comes from Sanskrit and, like Sanskrit, is written in **Devanagari**, which is derived from Brahmi, the earliest known writing system in India. Many other major languages too, like Bengali, Punjabi and Marathi, have writing systems that come from Devanagari.

The important languages of South India, like Tamil, Telugu, Kannada and Malayalam, are called Dravidian languages and are said to have originated right there in the southern peninsula. In very few places, mostly in the North-East, the Austro-Asiatic and Sino-Tibetan groups of languages are used.

## L for Languages

## IT'S OFFICIAL!

There are 22 'scheduled languages', that is, languages recognized by the Indian Constitution and used by states in their official work. They are: Assamese, Bengali, Bodo, Dogri, Gujarati, Hindi, Kannada, Kashmiri, Konkani, Maithili, Malayalam, Manipuri, Marathi, Nepali, Oriya, Punjabi, Sanskrit, Santhali, Sindhi, Tamil, Telugu and Urdu.

English, which was introduced by the British who once ruled our country, is an associate official language. In fact, India today has more English-speaking people than Great Britain. English continues to be used in Parliament along with Hindi, and by governments, businesses, schools, colleges, newspapers and television channels!

Certain ancient languages with a rich literary tradition such as Sanskrit, Tamil, Kannada, Malayalam, Oriya and Telugu have been declared classical languages by the Government of India.

## LANGUAGE RUCKUS

Hindi is the most widely spoken language in India, and in 1950, the Indian Constitution declared Hindi the official language of the country. But English was to be used along with Hindi for 15 years more. In 1965, when all the states were asked to switch over to Hindi, the non-Hindi speaking states, especially Tamil Nadu, agitated against the changeover, till they were assured that Hindi would not be imposed on them and that English would be retained as an associate language.

Six years after India became independent, the States Reorganization Commission was formed in 1953 to draw up state boundaries, broadly on the basis of language. Such a division of the country caused several problems, as many groups within each state felt that their language and culture had not been safeguarded. These communities are demanding new states for themselves!

WANNA COME?

VANAKKAM! SUB TICK TOCK?

I THOUGHT *PANINI* WAS JUST A TYPE OF SANDWICH!

## PANINI'S PRICELESS GIFT

Panini, who lived around 650 BCE, wrote the first grammar book in the world. He framed the rules of Sanskrit grammar according to scientific tenets. He has been called the father of descriptive linguistics (linguistics is the study of language). His methods were adopted not only by Western linguists but also in the field of computer languages!

# for Lucknow

This ancient city blossomed into the cultural capital of North India under the Nawabs of Avadh. It is renowned for its tradition of gracious hospitality, courtly etiquette and polished manners, and also for its mouth-watering kebabs, biriyani and rewadi. Welcome to Lucknow!

## FACT OR FICTION?

The story goes that Lord Rama, King of Ayodhya, gave some land to his brother Lakshman (who was also known as Lakhan), to build himself a city. This city came to be known as Lucknow.

Later, Lucknow was taken over by many rulers, including the Mughals, the Nawabs of Avadh, and then the British. The city, which became a part of the province of Avadh, starred in our freedom struggle too. After India got its Independence from British rule, Lucknow became the capital of the state of Uttar Pradesh.

A Lucknowi meal fit for royalty

## FREEDOM OR DEATH

Nawab Wajid Ali Shah of Avadh was totally engrossed in music, dance and poetry, and showed no interest in ruling his kingdom. This suited the British, and in 1856 they annexed Avadh, which was the key to controlling the fertile Gangetic plain. They also sent the nawab into exile.

This proved to be one of the causes for the uprising in 1857. The people were outraged and besieged the Residency. The British commissioner Henry Lawrence and other British citizens were rescued by British troops, five months later. Thousands were killed in the operation.

## LEGENDARY LUCKNOW

• Lucknow is dotted with magnificent monuments, such as the **Residency**, the walls of which still have bullet marks from the Siege of Lucknow, the **Bara Imambara** with its mysterious labyrinth of passages, the **Chota Imambara**, the **Rumi Darwaza** and the **Pearl Mosque**.

• One of Lucknow's most celebrated crafts is its delicate, traditional **chikan** hand-embroidery, which provides livelihood to thousands of people.

# for Metros

**They are a patchwork of the old and the new—ancient monuments, stunning skyscrapers, restaurants, malls, businesses and bazaars. They provide employment and entertainment to millions, rich and poor, and are political and cultural hubs. Welcome to the metropolitan cities—or metros—of India!**

## DAZZLING NEW DELHI

British architects Edwin Lutyens and Herbert Baker designed and built New Delhi. It was inaugurated as the capital of British India in 1931, and remained India's capital after Independence. It is now part of the National Capital Territory of Delhi, which also includes historic Old Delhi (this is chock-a-block with bazaars and magnificent monuments like the Red Fort and Jama Masjid, and was the capital of many great empires), and neighbouring areas like Faridabad, Gurgaon, Ghaziabad and so on.

**New Delhi is special because:**

• It is not only India's capital city, but also its administrative hub and home to the Indian Parliament, the Rashtrapati Bhavan (where the President stays) and the Supreme Court, besides government offices and embassies.

The Delhi Durbar of 1911, when the shifting of India's capital from Calcutta to Delhi was announced.

## MAGNIFICENT MUMBAI

Cosmopolitan Mumbai, the capital of Maharashtra, is not only our biggest and most crowded metro, but also one of the largest cities in the world. It is built on a group of seven islands in the Arabian Sea. It was once part of the territory captured by the Portuguese, and was given as dowry to King Charles II of England when he married Princess Catherine de Braganza of Portugal.

**Mumbai is special because:**

• It is the financial, commercial and entertainment hub of India.

• It hosts the largest cinema industry in the world—Bollywood.

• Its port is the biggest in India and handles almost half the cargo of the country.

• Mahatma Gandhi launched the Quit India Movement for independence from British rule here, in August 1942.

The sprawling city of Mumbai gets its name from Goddess Mumbadevi who, for centuries, has been worshipped by the people living here.

# for Metros

## KOLKATA KALEIDOSCOPE

What comes to mind when you hear the words rosogolla and Rabindra Sangeet, Howrah Bridge and Victoria Memorial? Kolkata, of course! From a tiny village on the bank of the Hooghly River, where an English merchant, Job Charnock, established a trading post in 1690, it grew into the bustling city of Calcutta (now Kolkata). It was the capital of British India from 1772–1911.

**Kolkata is special because:**

• It is the capital of West Bengal, and considered the cultural as well as literary capital of India.

• It had the longest-serving Communist government in the world, elected democratically by the people.

• Nobel Laureates Rabindranath Tagore, C.V. Raman and Amartya Sen have been associated with the city.

The iconic Victoria Memorial in Kolkata

## WHAT IS A METRO?

A metropolitan city is a city that has a large population (over 10 lakhs), while a metropolitan area includes such a city and the places around it from where people commute to the city for work, etc. **Delhi**, **Bombay** (now Mumbai), **Calcutta** (now Kolkata) and **Madras** (now Chennai) were the earliest to be called metropolitan cities, in India. Later, **Bangalore** and **Hyderabad**, India's IT hubs, got included, and more recently cities like **Ahmedabad**, **Pune**, **Visakhapatnam** and **Surat** have made the cut.

## CHENNAI CHATTER

It was in Chennai (then Madras) that the British established a settlement called Fort St George in 1639, and from this stronghold their power grew in the south. Even now, Chennai is called the Gateway to South India.

**Chennai is special because:**

• It is the capital of Tamil Nadu, and the automobile capital of India—40 per cent of the country's automobile industries are there.

• It is an important cultural centre, best known for the classical dance form Bharatnatyam and for its annual music festival.

• The city's Marina Beach is one of the longest urban beaches in the world.

There are numerous statues and memorials along the scenic Marina beach, which is one of the most crowded seafronts in the country.

# for Monsoon

**The monsoon is a spectacular sound-and-light show that begins in summer with thunder, lightning and stormy gusts of wind. Then, torrents of rain sweep across the country turning parched fields and forests green ... and sometimes causing deadly, destructive floods and disastrous landslides.**

The monsoons bring much-needed rain to the country.

## WHAT ARE THE MONSOONS?

The word 'monsoon' comes from the Arabic word 'mausim,' meaning season. The monsoons refer to seasonal winds and the heavy rains that accompany them. The monsoons bring rain to parts of Africa, Australia, the USA and Asia. But they affect India the most, for we get 90 per cent of our water from the monsoons, and farmers depend on the rains to grow their crops.

## WHAT CAUSES THE MONSOONS?

The powerful monsoon winds are linked to the seasons. They blow from colder to warmer regions because hot air is lighter and rises, and cool air rushes in to take its place. During summer, the land is hotter than the ocean and heats the air above it. So monsoon winds carrying moisture from the Indian Ocean surge across the subcontinent from the south-west, bringing heavy rain. In winter, when the land is cooler than the ocean, the monsoon winds blow from the north-east, from land to sea. The north-east monsoon gathers moisture from the Bay of Bengal and brings heavy rain to Andhra Pradesh and Tamil Nadu.

**Mawsynram** in the Khasi Hills of Meghalaya is the wettest place on earth and gets nearly 12 m of rain a year. This is followed closely by nearby **Cherrapunji**.

## RAINS TO THE RESCUE

In 326 BCE, Alexander the Great of Macedonia stormed into India on a conquering spree, vanquishing king after king . . . until the skies opened up. That's when River Beas became dangerously swollen with the monsoon rains. It was the last straw for his tired, homesick soldiers. They refused to cross the river to fight any further battles and Alexander had to turn back.

# M

## for Monuments

Dotted across India are many magnificent monuments and sites that tell tales of the country's glorious past. They include castles, forts, temples, churches, towers, observatories, tombs and more.

Many of our monuments, including superstars like the **Taj Mahal** (Page 133), **Red Fort** (Page 40), **Jantar Mantar** (Page 100), **Qutub Mina**r (Page 116), the **churches of Goa** (Page 15) and the **Chola temples** (Page 134) are on the World Heritage List of the United Nations Educational and Scientific Organization (UNESCO). This means they are of great cultural and historical importance to people all over the world. So the government is taking special steps to protect them and others on the list, such as the following:

## KONARK SUN TEMPLE

On the seashore in Konark, Orissa, stands the gigantic Sun Temple built in the 13th century CE. It is in the form of the chariot of Surya, the Sun God, and has 24 exquisitely carved wheels, representing the 24 hours of the day. It was once drawn by seven horses (now there are six), one for each day of the week.

The Sun Temple was partly destroyed in the 16th century by the Muslim invader Kalapahad. At first his men were unable to break this magnificent stone structure. So Kalapahad had them remove the supporting pillars and the keystone at the top, which kept everything together. Sure enough, portions of the temple collapsed.

*Exquisite carvings at the Khajuraho Temple*

*The Konark Temple gets its name from the Sun God, who is also called Konaditya and Arka.*

## KHAJURAHO TEMPLES

Like the Konark Sun Temple, the temples at Khajuraho in Madhya Pradesh (built by the Chandelas in the 10th and 11th centuries) are covered with superb carvings of gods and goddesses, people and animals. However, these monuments too fell into ruin. Now, both Konark and Khajuraho have been spruced up by the government and buzz with tourists especially during the famous dance festivals held there every year.

# for Monuments

## FATEHPUR SIKRI

Fatehpur Sikri (the City of Victory) in Uttar Pradesh was built in the 16th century by Emperor Akbar to celebrate his victory in Gujarat. Akbar founded it on the site where the saint Salim Chisti predicted the birth of his son Jahangir. The most notable monuments there are Salim Chisti's tomb, the Jama Masjid, India's biggest mosque, which can hold 10,000 people, and its renowned gateway, Buland Darwaza (meaning high gate or gate of magnificence), which is decorated with pillars, turrets and carvings. It is 15 storeys high and one of the largest gateways in the world.

The imposing Buland Darwaza at Fatehpur Sikri

## BHIMBETKA ROCK SHELTERS

At the foot of the Vindhya Mountains in Bhimbetka, Madhya Pradesh, are five clusters of natural rock shelters with dazzling Stone Age paintings. Some of these are 30,000 years old and swarm with people who hunt and dance and do their daily chores. And there are animals too, like deer, elephants, crocodiles, tigers and lions—running, charging, fighting.

It is said that the mighty Pandava warrior Bhima (from the epic Mahabharata) had visited the region, for the name 'Bhimbetka' means sitting place of Bhima.

The beautiful Shore Temple at Mahabalipuram

## CAVE TEMPLES

Cave temples, which are hundreds of years old, are scattered across the country. These are covered with exquisite rock-cut carvings based on Hindu, Buddhist and Jain religious scriptures. Some of the best ones are in Maharashtra at **Ajanta** and **Ellora** and on the island of **Elephanta**, near Mumbai. No one knows how ancient people with their primitive tools created these amazing monuments and sculptures, but legends say that the Pandava superheroes did it all. **Mahabalipuram** or Mamallapuram in Tamil Nadu has colossal monuments with important scenes from the Mahabharata cut from rock. It is also famous for its Shore Temple, and a bas relief (raised sculpture on a flat stone background) that is 100 feet long!

# for Monuments

## THE STUPAS OF SANCHI

Like the Mahabodhi Temple in Bodh Gaya, Bihar, the stupas (mound-like structures where relics are kept) at Sanchi in Madhya Pradesh are sacred to Buddhists. There are four toranas or gateways around the stupas, which are covered with sculptures of scenes from the life of Buddha and his miracles. The toranas stand for love, peace, trust and courage, respectively. Sanchi flourished from the time of Emperor Ashoka (3rd century BCE) to the 12th century CE. The important monuments there include monasteries, temples, gateways, pillars and stupas. Sanchi's Great Stupa is one of the oldest stone monuments in India.

The Great Stupa at Sanchi, which is part of a complex of ancient Buddhist structures.

## THE REMAINS OF HAMPI

Hampi was the capital of the fabled Vijaynagar Empire (in Karnataka) where precious gems were sold like grains in the marketplace. It was known for its bazaars and markets, its art and culture, for its temples like the Vittala Temple with its musical pillars and for buildings like the Lotus Mahal. The empire reached great heights between the 14th and 16th centuries. But Muslim invaders who conquered the kingdom after the Battle of Talikota in 1565 destroyed the city, plundered it for six months, and left it in ruins. Yet, its monuments are so impressive that tourists still flock to Hampi to view what's left of them.

## CHHATRAPATI SHIVAJI TERMINUS

It has been said that Mumbai's **Victoria Terminus** (popularly known as VT) is to the British Raj what the Taj Mahal is to the Mughal Empire. VT, now renamed Chhatrapati Shivaji Terminus, is the busiest railway station in India. It is a grand old Gothic building with towers, turrets, arches, domes and carvings, which beautifully blends the Victorian and Mughal styles of architecture. The station was designed by Frederick William Stevens, and named in honour of Queen Victoria, during whose Golden Jubilee in 1887 it was opened. In November 2008, a deadly terrorist attack on the station left 58 people dead and several badly injured.

The ruins of the legendary city of Hampi, capital of the Vijayanagar Empire

# for Musical Instruments

**The earliest musical instruments were sticks and stones, conches, shells and bones. Later, people also made music with pots and pans and reeds!**

## THE MUSIC OF THE GODS

Many ancient musical instruments are still used in classical and folk music. And some of these, such as drums, cymbals and bells, play an important role in religious ceremonies and are also associated with the divine. It is said that when Lord Krishna played his flute, animals, birds and people were drawn to him by the magic of his music, and even rivers stopped flowing to listen to him!

## VAST VARIETY

Indian musical instruments fall into three broad categories: stringed instruments, wind instruments and percussion instruments. The stringed instruments usually have a wooden body and strings, and music is played by vibrating the strings with the fingers or with a bow.

Some of the popular stringed instruments in India are the **veena**, **sitar**, **santoor**, **sarod**, **tanpura**, **dilruba** and **sarangi**. The oldest of these is the veena, which is mentioned in ancient Hindu scriptures such as the Ramayana and the Puranas. The veena is said to be a favourite of Saraswati, Goddess of Learning. Lord Shiva, Sage Narada and even Ravana, the king of Lanka, were accomplished veena players!

The other popular stringed instrument in the subcontinent is the **sitar**. It even travelled to the West in the 1950s after the Beatles, the iconic pop music group at the time, learnt to play it from the accomplished sitar maestro, Ravi Shankar, and included it in their concerts and performances.

Ravi Shankar

## ALL-TIME GREATS

Sitar: **Vilayat Khan, Ravi Shankar**
Sarod: **Amjad Ali Khan**

# M for Musical Instruments

Wind instruments are usually in the form of a long tube and produce music when air is blown through or across an opening in the tube. By controlling the breath, various tunes can be played on them. The most popular wind instruments in the country are the **shehnai**, **nadaswaram** and **flute**.

The bold, loud nadaswaram of South India and its counterpart, the shehnai, of North India, are considered most auspicious. They are played during marriages, temple ceremonies, and religious gatherings.

*A nadaswaram player (on the right) accompanied by a tavil player*

## ALL-TIME GREATS

Shehnai: **Bismillah Khan**

Nadaswaram: **Sheikh Chinna Moulana Sahib**

Flute: **Hariprasad Chaurasia**

Bismillah Khan

Percussion instruments like the **tabla**, **mridangam**, **damru** and **dholak** are hot favourites in this country. Go for these if you like to strike, rattle or shake things in order to make music.

Most Indian percussion instruments are made of wood or metal and tightly stretched animal skin, and many of these go way back in time. In fact, ancient Hindu scriptures mention deities like Ganesha playing the **mridangam**. The mridangam's North Indian musical counterpart is the **tabla**—a pair of drums—used in Hindustani classical and devotional music. The name 'tabla' comes, from the Arabic word, 'tabl', which means drum.

There are some other amazing percussion instruments, which do not use animal skin, such as the **ghatam**, popular in South India. It is a mud pot with a narrow mouth, which the musician holds against his tummy and taps with flying fingers to make music.

Then there is the **jalatarangam**, which consists of porcelain cups of different sizes, arranged in a semicircle before the performer. Water is poured into the cups, and the quantity is adjusted to get the right pitch. The cups are struck with two thin sticks, and it's music, music, music . . . so long as the player doesn't get thirsty and go glug, glug, glug!

## ALL-TIME GREATS

Mridangam: **Palghat Mani Iyer**

Tabla: **Zakir Hussain, Qureshi Alla Rakha**

## for Mythical Monsters

They come in startling shapes and sizes. Many of them are champion magicians who fly, become invisible, create illusions, and turn into humans, animals or monsters. Indian mythology is full of these spine-chilling beings—big, bad and bizarre!

## GRAVE GAMES

The **vetala**, **bhoot**, **chudail**, **pishacha** and **preta** are some of our most blood-curdling ghosts and ghouls, fiends and vampires. People believe that they hang around tamarind trees and graveyards (sometimes upside down, and with their legs never ever touching the ground), cast no shadows, slurp the blood of unwary humans who stray into their neighbourhood and snack on human flesh.

## THE TERRIBLE THREE

In ancient times, there were the **asuras** and **rakshasas** whose favourite pastime was wrecking the pujas of the sages and terrorizing people everywhere. Here are a few examples:

The ever-hungry **Bakasura** would go on a rampage unless he was provided with a cartload of food every day. And this ravenous rakshasa would gobble it all—cart, goodies, driver and bullocks! One day, Bhima (one of the Pandavas in the Mahabharata), who had been assigned to take the asura his food, sat down and began to eat it himself! Bakasura was so furious he charged forward bellowing. In the fight that followed, he was killed by Bhima.

The wicked demon **Mahishasura** could turn himself into a super buffalo, mighty as a mountain, whenever he wished. He prayed long and hard till he was granted a boon that no man could ever slay him, and soon, he was able to conquer the three worlds. But in the end, a woman—a form of Goddess Durga known as Katyayani or Chamundi—came into battle riding a tiger and killed him!

Then there was the asura **Raktabija** who had been granted a terrifying boon. With every drop of his blood that fell on the battlefield, another Raktabija clone rose up to fight his enemies. Eventually, in the course of a fierce battle, Goddess Kali drank the blood falling from the asura's body, making sure not even a single drop touched the ground. This helped Goddess Durga kill him.

# for Mythical Monsters

## SLITHER AND STRIKE

Giants snakes, both good and evil, play a huge role in Indian mythology. **Anantha** or **Adisesha**, a mighty serpent with 1000 heads is said to wear the entire universe like a crown on his hood.

During the time of Lord Krishna, the gigantic seven-headed serpent **Kaliya** or **Kalinga** had made River Yamuna his home, poisoning the water and burning up the grass on its banks. The people complained to Krishna, who jumped into the river, climbed on top of Kaliya's hood and danced fiercely on it, draining the snake of all his power.

Ever heard of eco-friendly snakes? Well, the **naginis** were female spirits who often took the form of snakes. They lived near the water and punished humans who polluted the environment, by covering their skin with boils. They also rewarded responsible citizens by blessing their crops!

## MIGHTY MIXED UP

Not all rakshasas were entirely gross and wicked. In fact, the mightiest and most powerful of them all, the terrible ten-headed **Ravana**, king of Lanka, was a skilled musician. He was also very well-read in the scriptures. His long reign of evil ended when he was killed in battle by Lord Rama.

Ravana's brother **Kumbhakarna** had prayed for many years until Brahma the Creator granted him a boon. Kumbhakarna wished to demand the destruction of the devas (gods). But through a slip of the tongue, he ended up asking for the boon of long-lasting sleep. So he went snore-snore-SNORE for months. When Ravana wanted Kumbhakarna to help him in the war against Rama, Kumbhakarna finally woke up only after 1000 elephants walked over him. And then, he tried in vain to persuade his brother to do the right thing and allow Sita to return to her husband Rama!

# for Namaste

**In various parts of the world, people greet each other by hugging, shaking hands, or even rubbing noses. But in India, on the streets, in trains and planes, and at gatherings big and small, you are sure to hear one traditional greeting—Namaste.**

## KNOW YOUR NAMASTE

'Namaste' and its variations 'namaskar' and 'namaskaram' are greetings used by Hindus, Jains and Buddhists to greet young and old, family and friends or even total strangers. Want to try it? Just bend your elbows, join your palms together, facing upwards, in front of your chest, flash a warm, friendly smile and say 'Namaste!'

The word 'namaste' comes from Sanskrit and means 'I bow to you,' acknowledging that everyone is equal and worthy of being saluted. The joining of the palms symbolically says 'May our minds meet'.

The namaste has travelled everywhere, especially to the countries of South-East Asia. In Japan it is called 'gassho' and is mostly used in prayer.

KONYUNE ONORANGE TANKA?

## GREETINGS GALORE

Various communities in India have their special salutations too. When they meet, Muslims say 'Salaam' or 'Assalaam Aleikum' (Peace be upon you). Sikhs greet one another with the words, 'Sat Sri Akal' (God is the final Truth). The namaste is not the only greeting used by Hindus. Across the country, the other popular ones are, 'Hari Om' and 'Ram Ram'. The English 'hello' has also crept into some Indian languages in a desi disguise, for instance, as 'hailo' in Punjabi.

If you'd rather say, 'How are you?' when you greet someone, get set to pick from phrases such as these: Kemon acchen? (Bengali), Tame kem chho? (Gujarati), Hegiddhira? (Kannada), Sukhamaano? (Malayalam), Nwng mabwrwi dong? (Bodo), Aap kaise hain? (Hindi)

*The traditional namaste*

## GET NOSEY

Follow the lead of the Onge who live in the Andaman Islands and say, 'Konyune onorange tanka?' It's a general greeting, which translates as 'How is your nose?' Now isn't that cool?

# N for National Parks

**India's national parks are home to thousands of species of plants and animals, and play a huge role in their conservation.**

## SAVE US, SAVE THE WORLD!

In India, wild animals, birds and plants are protected under the **Wildlife Protection Act, 1972**. Hey, this is not a cool new thing. Way back in the 3rd century BCE, Emperor Ashoka gave up hunting, ordered his people to treat animals with kindness, and passed laws to protect wildlife and forests!

The tiger, India's national animal

## TIGER, TIGER, BURNING BRIGHT

Sure there are laws to protect wildlife, but poachers break them, time and again, hunting elephants for their tusks, rhinos for their horns, tigers for their skin, bones and teeth, and other animals for various reasons. Their numbers are dwindling and many species are in danger of dying out altogether. So the government has come up with various measures, like **Project Tiger** and **Project Elephant**, to protect and conserve these endangered animals.

**The Corbett National Park** in Uttaranchal was the first to come under Project Tiger. Some of the other important tiger reserves are:

**Bandhavgarh**, famous for its white tigers

**Sundarbans**, also known for its crocodiles

**Kanha**, which also has other stars like leopards, bears and various kinds of deer

**Dudhwa**, where the rare swamp deer or barasingha are found, and

**Ranthambore**, where there are tigers with crazy names like Slant Ear, Broken Tail and even a huge one called Baccha (Baby)!

Along with tigers, there are elephants too at **Bandipur** and **Periyar**, but if you're looking for a tiger-elephant-rhino combo with pythons, wild buffaloes and barasingha sunning themselves, your best bet would be **Manas** or **Kaziranga** in Assam.

If your favourite animal is the king of the jungle, you have to visit the **Gir National Park** in Gujarat. It has the last of the Asiatic lions in the whole wide world!

# N for National Parks

## BIRDS AND BEASTS

If you love colourful creatures that crawl, fly, slither or sing, Rajasthan's **Keoladeo Ghana National Park** (also known as the **Bharatpur Bird Sanctuary**, which, by the way, is the largest bird sanctuary in Asia) is the place for you.

This man-made park was created by the Maharaja of Bharatpur and named after the ancient Keoladeo (Shiva) temple there, and the ghana (thick) forests. Soon thousands of migratory birds began to arrive at the park, in winter, from as far away as Central Asia and Siberia.

**Main Attractions**: Siberian cranes, pelicans, boars, snakes, deer

Want to catch a glimpse of the endangered Great Indian Bustard, found only in India? Then make a trip to the **Desert National Park** in the Thar Desert, Rajasthan, the biggest desert in the country.

Siberian cranes fly more than 6400 km to come to India in winter.

The snow leopard has long been hunted for its fur and has now become an endangered species.

## HEAD FOR THE HEIGHTS

The top two high-altitude national parks are in the state of Jammu and Kashmir. The **Dachigam National Park**, amidst the Himalayas is home to the state animal, the endangered hangul, the only species of red deer in India. But if you're on the trail of the elusive snow leopard, then huff and puff to the largest national park in India, Ladakh's **Hemis High Altitude National Park**.

**Other Stars**: musk deer, Himalayan brown bear, leopard, golden eagle

## DIVE TO THE DEPTHS

Looking for a water wonderland, where dugongs and porpoises come to play? Then take off for the country's first **Marine National Park**, which is in the Gulf of Kutch off the coast of Gujarat.

You can even travel south to the **Gulf of Mannar Marine National Park** along the coast of Tamil Nadu. The park is dotted with islands and coral reefs, marshes and mangroves. To protect the endangered species there, like whales, dugongs and dolphins, visitors are allowed to explore the park only by going on glass-bottom boat rides.

# for National Symbols

Our national symbols are special because they encourage people to bond together in a spirit of patriotism. They also reflect our country's history, tradition and values. Here are a few fun facts about them . . .

## NATIONAL FLAG

Every independent nation in the world has this symbol of freedom—its very own flag. The national flag of India was designed by Pingali Venkayya and adopted in its present form on 22 July 1947 by the Constituent Assembly, a few days before India became a free country.

Guess why the Indian flag is called 'tiranga' or tricolour. That's easy-peasy . . . because it has three horizontal stripes! The saffron on top stands for courage and sacrifice, the white in the middle for truth and purity, and the green below for peace and prosperity. On the white stripe is the Dharma Chakra or the Wheel of Law with 24 spokes, representing justice and progress. This is taken from Emperor Ashoka's Lion Capital at Sarnath.

Nobel Laureate Rabindranath Tagore

## NATIONAL ANTHEM

Millions have stood at attention to this rousing song in honour of God and the motherland. It is our very own *Jana Gana Mana,* composed by Gurudev Rabindranath Tagore. This was adopted as the national anthem of India when the country became a Republic in 1950. It takes less than a minute to sing. Yet it has inspired generations of Indians, because of its vision of an India where people of different races, religions and languages unite together as patriots.

## NATIONAL EMBLEM

The national emblem is also adapted from the same Lion Capital. It has three lions symbolizing courage, pride and confidence. Below that are the Dharma Chakra and the motto, 'Satyameva Jayate,' which means truth alone triumphs.

सत्यमेव जयते

## NATIONAL SONG

Another song that thrilled and unified the country during the freedom struggle was Bankim Chandra Chatterjee's *Vande Mataram.* It is now our national song.

## NATIONAL ANIMAL

It is the largest animal in the cat family and the only one with orange, black and white stripes. This strong, graceful creature darts swiftly through the forest and can kill even a young elephant or rhino with a leap and a bite. Meet the tiger or *Panthera tigris*, India's national animal.

Tigers are fast disappearing although most countries, including India, have laws for their protection. But people continue to hunt them, and are destroying the forests where the felines live.

The tiger is known for its grace, intelligence and strength.

### STRIPE HYPE

Did you know you can tell tigers apart by their stripes because each tiger has a different pattern?

The peacock is found in forests and fields all over the Indian subcontinent.

## NATIONAL BIRD

What could possibly be the national bird of a country like ours, where all the colours you see are bright and beautiful? The proud, graceful peacock or *Pavo cristatus*, of course!

Surprise! Surprise! The male has a shimmering blue body, and tail feathers of blue, green, gold and bronze, dotted with 'eyes'. He arches these into a spectacular fan to attract females, which are a drab, dull brown!

### OUR NATIONAL BIRD ROCKS!

The peacock is a terrific dancer. No wonder a group of peacocks is called a **party**!

## NATIONAL RIVER

Our national river is the Ganga, the longest river in India and the most sacred river of the Hindus.

## NATIONAL SPORT

Field hockey is our national sport. India holds a record of eight Olympic gold medals in this game.

# N

### for National Symbols

## NATIONAL CALENDAR

The Saka calendar begins with a historical event—King Salivahana's accession to the throne in 79 CE. So that makes it the 1st year of the Saka calendar, which was adopted as our national calendar in 1957.

## NATIONAL FLOWER

Our national flower, the lotus or *Nelumbo nucifera*, is considered sacred by Hindus, Buddhists and Jains, and is associated with several deities. It is a symbol of purity for although the lotus plant grows in slushy water, the flowers rise above it without getting muddy.

## NATIONAL TREE

The Banyan or *Ficus bengalensis*, which often figures in our myths, grows all over the country. It is our national tree and is considered a symbol of the nation's unity. In smaller towns and villages, panchayat meetings are often held in its cool shade.

The mango is called the king of fruits.

## NATIONAL FRUIT

Sindhura, Aruna, Mallika . . . these are some of the stars whom you can meet without stepping into a theatre, for they are all sweet, juicy mangoes, as are the Alphonso, Rasburi, Dassehri and hundreds of other varieties in different shapes, sizes and colours.

Do you know why scientists call the mango tree *Mangifera indica*? The tree first appeared in India some 5000 years ago and was then grown in other countries. The word 'mango' comes from the Tamil word 'mangai' and India is the largest grower of mangoes in the world. The fruit was such a huge favourite with the Mughal Emperor Akbar that he planted 1,00,000 mango trees in Darbhanga, Bihar, which still flourish at a place now known as Lakhi Bagh.

The mango is often called the king of fruits. So is it any wonder that it is the national fruit of India?

### STRANGE BUT TRUE

In the ancient Ekambareswarar Temple in Kanchipuram there is a sacred mango tree, and each of its four branches bears an entirely different kind of mango!

The banyan tree is found all over India, and lives for hundreds of years.

# N for Newspapers

Newspapers bring us articles, advertisements, cartoons, crosswords and lots of news, of course, to shape the way we think. Psst! They can also be used to make paper cones for fried groundnuts and channa!

Over 200 years ago, the printing press was first introduced in India by Portuguese and British missionaries, who wished to print pamphlets in order to spread Christianity. But the press soon became a powerful tool in the hands of several freedom fighters like Gandhiji (who published *Nav Jeevan*, *Young India* and *Harijan*), Bal Gangadhar Tilak (who published *Kesari*), and Raja Ram Mohan Roy (who brought out magazines in English, Hindi, Persian and Bengali). They used the press to shape public opinion, which is why Indian newspapers played a huge role during the freedom struggle. They also helped in bringing about social reforms by tackling questions such as child marriage, education for women and sati.

CAN YOU BELIEVE THERE WAS A TIME WHEN THERE WAS NO TV? PEOPLE HAD TO *READ* TO GET THE NEWS!

## PAPA OF THE INDIAN PRESS

The first Indian newspaper in English, the *Bengal Gazette*, was started by an Irishman, **James Augustus Hickey**, in 1780. The paper was the size of a notebook, and he used it to attack the corrupt and people he disliked, including British Governor General Warren Hastings, who had him thrown into prison. But he continued to publish his newspaper from jail until his printing machine was taken away. That was the end of the paper, and Hickey died a pauper.

## DID YOU KNOW?

• **Calcutta** was the birthplace of English, Bengali, Hindi and Urdu newspapers.

• *Samachar Darpan* in Bengali, published in 1818, was the first newspaper in an Indian language.

• The countries with the world's highest newspaper circulation are China, India and Japan.

• The **Press Trust of India** (PTI) is India's largest news agency. It collects and provides news to newspapers as well as to radio and television companies.

• The *Times of India* is the largest selling English newspaper in the whole world!

# N for Nobel Laureates

What is the most prestigious award for outstanding contributions 'to the good of humanity' in the fields of physics, chemistry, medicine, literature, peace and economics? Yes, it's the Nobel Prize, an award established by the Swedish chemist Alfred Nobel who invented dynamite.

Noble souls and Nobel Laureates . . . India has them all! Four celebrated Indian citizens and six others with Indian roots have been awarded the Nobel Prize. Ready for some superstar surprises?

GO INDIA!

## INCREDIBLE INDIANS

**RABINDRANATH TAGORE (1861–1941)**
**Awarded the Nobel Prize for Literature in 1913** for *Gitanjali*

### Isn't This Amazing!
• He was a philosopher, poet, songwriter, playwright, novelist and painter . . . and the first Asian to be awarded the Nobel Prize.

• He founded Vishva-Bharati, a famous university, and an amazing school at Santiniketan, where classes were held outdoors so that learning was more like exploration and fun.

• The national anthems of both India and Bangladesh were composed by him.

**C.V. RAMAN (1888–1970)**
**Awarded the Nobel Prize for Physics in 1930** for his discovery called the Raman Effect, about certain properties of light.

### Isn't This Amazing!
• He joined college at the age of 11 and graduated at the top of his class!

• He was associated with some of India's best-known educational and research institutions such as the Indian Institute of Science and the Raman Research Institute, both in Bangalore.

• His research spanned sound, light, crystals and the functioning of the human eye.

*Amartya Sen, whose economic theories focus on the welfare of the poor and the disadvantaged*

**AMARTYA SEN (born in 1933)**
**Awarded the Nobel Prize for Economics in 1998** for his contribution to welfare economics, especially his studies on famine, and how to improve the condition of women and the poor.

### Isn't This Amazing!
• Sen believes that the government can and should help even the poorest citizens to live better lives. How? By making sure that the country's resources are distributed fairly.

# N for Nobel Laureates

*Mother Teresa, who was called the Saint of the Gutters*

**MOTHER TERESA (1910–1997)**
**Awarded the Nobel Peace Prize in 1979**
for her humanitarian work among the poor

### Isn't This Amazing!

• She became a nun as a young girl and left her home in Skopje, Macedonia, to work among the poorest of the poor in the slums of Calcutta (now Kolkata). There, she wished to start a school, but had no money, no companions, no help. She quietly picked up a stick and wrote the letters of the Bengali alphabet in the mud. A few children gathered around her. And believe it or not, it slowly grew into a real school!

• It was Mother Teresa's belief that our life is like a lamp, and small deeds and words of kindness are the tiny drops of oil that make it burn.

• She founded the Missionaries of Charity, a group of nuns who helped her look after the sick and homeless in several countries.

## FOREIGN CITIZENS, INDIAN CONNECTIONS

Some Nobel Laureates such as these had Indian roots, but were citizens of other countries when they received the Nobel Prize:

**Har Gobind Khorana**
Year: **1968** Subject: **Medicine** (for his study of how genes within a cell affect the way the cell works)
Citizen of: **USA**

**Subrahmanyan Chandrasekhar**
Year: **1983** Subject: **Physics** (for his research on how stars evolve)
Citizen of: **USA**

**V.S. Naipaul**
Year: **2001** Subject: **Literature** (for a large body of work that includes novels and non-fiction)
Citizen of: **UK**

**Venkatraman Ramakrishnan**
Year: **2009** Subject: **Chemistry** (for his research on ribsomes, which help cells to process the proteins needed for our growth)
Citizen of: **USA**

**Ronald Ross**
Year: **1902** Subject: **Medicine** (for his research on malaria)
Citizen of: **UK**

**Rudyard Kipling**
Year: **1907** Subject: **Literature** (for his wonderful poetry and imaginative fiction, which includes works like *The Jungle Book*)
Citizen of: **UK**

MERA BHARAT MAHAAN!

# O for Observatories

An observatory is a building from which astronomers study the stars, planets and galaxies. But over 250 years ago, there were spectacular observatories of another kind in India, such as these ...

A view of the colossal 18th century observatory, Jantar Mantar, in Delhi

## JANTAR MANTAR

In the early 18th century, the Mughal Emperor Muhammad Shah was once setting out on an important expedition. The court astrologers were, however, involved in a huge debate about the auspicious time to begin the journey. Maharaja Jai Singh of Rajasthan, who was a learned astronomer, happened to notice this ruckus. He came up with a smart plan to put an end to such yelling matches. With the emperor's permission, he began to build an observatory in Delhi to study the skies and prepare accurate astronomical tables. Why? Because auspicious dates were fixed depending on the movement of the planets.

The observatory was called Jantar Mantar, which means instrument for calculation. Jai Singh built five such observatories. The largest is in Jaipur and has colossal instruments of masonry and stone to measure the position of the sun, stars and planets.

The biggest of these instruments is the **Samrat Yantra** for telling the time. It is 90 feet tall and is the largest sundial in the world.

## PLANETS AND PRAYERS

Nowadays, scientists work in observatories. But during the time of Maharaja Jai Singh, learned priests ran the show! Whenever their calculations forecast an eclipse or monsoon rains, this was announced from a domed platform on top of the Samrat Yantra.

## PETRIE'S PRIDE

Modern astronomy and telescopes to observe the skies came to India with the British. The first important observatory was built in Madras in 1786. William Petrie, who worked for the British government, spent his own money and bought instruments to set up an observatory in his garden. This went on to become the **Madras Observatory**.

# O for Observatories

## THE CHIEF DOES IT ALL

There was a severe famine in the Madras Presidency in 1876–77. So the British, who ruled much of India at the time, decided to set up the **Kodaikanal Observatory** to study the sun and its effect on the monsoons. But there was a major hitch. Michie Smith, who was to head the institution, could not find any skilled workmen to build the special domes of the observatory. Hmm . . . no problem. He climbed up the towers and erected the domes, hammering in some 2300 rivets all by himself!

The Kodaikanal Observatory (established in 1899) is one of three solar observatories in the world that are over 75 years old. And it is still going strong!

## FATHER OF MODERN INDIAN ASTRONOMY

M.K. Vainu Bappu (1927–1982) was one of India's most brilliant astronomers. As a young boy, he dreamed of stars, planets and galaxies, and even discovered a comet while he was still a student. Vainu Bappu spent his life building telescopes and setting up astronomical institutes and observatories, like the prestigious one in Kavalur, Tamil Nadu. This has been named the **Vainu Bappu Observatory (VBO)** in his honour. For VBO, he undertook the tough task of building a huge telescope for research on stars and the solar system. In fact, this is the largest telescope in Asia, and it was built in India!

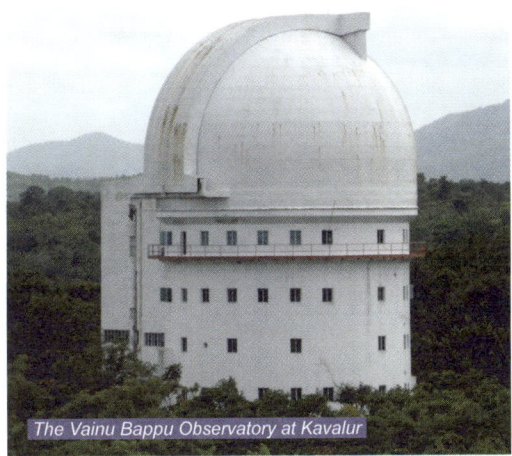

*The Vainu Bappu Observatory at Kavalur*

## EYE IN THE SKY

India has some of the most powerful telescopes in the world like the made-in-India **Giant Metrewave Radio Telescope (GMRT)** in Pune. The country also has excellent observatories in Udaipur, Ooty, Nainital, Mount Abu and Gauribidanur. But do you know why scientists from various parts of the world make a beeline for the **Indian Astronomical Observatory** at Hanle, in Ladakh? At 4500 m above sea level, it is one of the highest observatories in the world.

# O
## for Olive Ridley Turtles

**Millions of marine animals have made the oceans their home for centuries. But over time, people and their activities have driven some of these species to extinction, while others like the sea turtles, which have been around for 100 million years, are now in big trouble.**

An Olive ridley turtle resting on the beach after a long swim across the ocean

## TURTLE TRICKS

Of all the species of sea turtles, the smallest are the Olive ridley turtles. They are found in the Atlantic, Pacific and Indian Oceans. But these gentle reptiles are rapidly dwindling in numbers and are on the endangered list.

Do you know what Olive ridleys are famous for? Their mass nesting on the beaches. In Spanish, this is called 'arribada'. India has the largest turtle nesting site in the world. Around 6,00,000 turtles come to Orissa, at Gahirimatha, and at the mouth of the rivers, Devi and Rushikulya for this. The females return to the beach where they were born to lay their eggs. And they swim thousands of kilometres to get there! Don't ask how they know where to turn left or right . . .

## ISN'T THAT STRANGE!

Each female lays a huge clutch of 80 to 140 eggs at a time. So why isn't the earth overrun with Olive ridleys? Hungry eagles, crows, jackals, dogs and even human beings gobble up the eggs and baby turtles. So for every 1000 turtles just one survives.

The Olive ridley turtle gets its name from **F.N. Ridley**, the man who first spotted it in Brazil, and from the colour of its shell, which is olive green.

An Olive ridley nesting site

## DANGER AND DEATH

In Orissa, the World Wildlife Fund (WWF) has managed to get the local fishermen involved in protecting the Olive ridley nesting sites from predatory animals. But they are still being destroyed because of human activities. For instance, the trawlers and fishing nets kill around 1,00,000 turtles a year.

# for Olive Ridley Turtles

## GOING, GOING ...

Like the Olive ridley turtles, other marine species such as the ones listed below are endangered. This is mainly because of poaching, pollution and the destruction of coastal areas by people in the name of development. Or the propellers of big fishing boats go chop, chop, and the poor wounded animals bleed to death. Some of the marine animals that are in danger are:

The **gharial**, a crocodile with a thin, long snout that has a bulb at the end. Gharials once roamed the rivers of Bangladesh, North India, Nepal and Pakistan. But they were hunted for their skin. And now there are just 1200 of them left.

The **Ganges River Dolphin**, whose habitat has been damaged by the many dams that have been built across the rivers where the species lives. That's why their numbers have now dwindled to barely 1800.

The **Ganges Shark** lives in River Ganga and the Bay of Bengal. People kill them for their meat and oil.

The **whale shark** is found off the coast of Gujarat. They are so gentle that they sometimes play with divers and allow them to ride on their back. Sadly, they too are slaughtered for their flesh.

Various types of sea turtles from the smallest, the **Olive ridley turtle**, to the largest, the **Leatherback turtle**, which weighs almost 900 kg, are in danger. They are killed for their shells, meat and eggs, and are also used as bait and fertilizer!

The **dugong** or **sea cow** is found near the Gulf of Kutch and the Gulf of Mannar. These harmless herbivorous animals are hunted for their meat, skin, bones and oil.

## STOP THE SLAUGHTER

Under India's **Wildlife Protection Act, 1972**, the government has established wildlife sanctuaries, biosphere reserves and national parks to protect and conserve species that are in danger, including Olive ridley turtles.

## for Om

You will find it in different colours, sizes and forms—in rangolis, in puja decorations, wedding invitations, yoga books, and even on designer T-shirts. It is the symbol Om, sacred to Hindus, Buddhists and Jains.

## COOL TOOL!

Want to write the symbol Om but don't know how? Well, it looks a bit like the number there with some extra flourishes, like this:

Still can't figure it out? Never mind. Go to Microsoft Word on your computer. Open the Font box, select Wingdings, and just type the backslash ( \ ). Hey, there's your Om!

Would you like to chant it instead? Om is made up of the three sounds a-u-m, with 'a' and 'u' combining to become 'o'. Sit straight. Close your eyes and take a deep breath. As you breathe out, start chanting Om, very slowly. Focus and feel the vibration of the sound move from your navel to your throat and then to the top of your head.

## OM IN ORBIT

Do you know that the astronaut Sunita Williams carried with her a picture of the symbol Om during a recent space mission for NASA?

That's not the only time the emblem has been up above the world so high. There is a mountain peak in the Himalayas called **Om Parvat**. Why is it named so? Because the snow falling on it forms a pattern that resembles the symbol Om. According to legend, there are eight such spots in the world, but this is the only one that has been found until now.

## OMNIPRESENT OM

Modern science tells us that we and the rest of the universe are bundles of energy vibrating in various patterns. Depending on these patterns, you are a person, book, cat, and so on. The ancient Indian sages believed in something similar. Before the universe was created, there was just sound energy in the form of the word Om. And the entire universe developed from its vibrations.

# for Paintings

From ancient rock paintings to the masterpieces of modern art such as the works of M. F. Hussain, India has them all. Almost every region of the country has developed its own style of art, with religion and culture playing a huge role in shaping most of them.

## ROCK PAINTINGS ROCK

The cave paintings or murals are the earliest form of art in India, and those found at **Bhimbetka** (Page 85) are thousands of years old. Want to check out some other spectacular murals? Then head for the rock-cut caves of **Ajanta** and **Ellora** (Page 3).

The art of the **Warlis**, a tribe in Maharashtra, is similar to the Bhimbetka cave paintings. Using geometric shapes such as triangles, circles and squares, women paint birds, animals, trees and people on the walls of their homes. The Warli paintings are usually done in white on earthen walls. The 'paint' is rice paste and gum, and their 'brushes' are chewed bamboo sticks!

*Amazing cave paintings at Bhimbetka*

## MIRROR, MIRROR, ON THE WALL

In Rajasthan too, women paint pictures on the inside of their mud houses. The paintings are then studded with small mirrors. Can you guess why? Earlier, when they had no electricity, the single lamp that they lit would be reflected in all the mirrors. So it would brighten up the whole house. How clever is that!

*Glittering Tanjore paintings on display*

## SOUTHERN SENSATIONS

**Tanjore painting** from Thanjavur district in Tamil Nadu dates back to the 9th century, and is the most exquisite style of painting in South India. Hindu deities and legends about them form the subject of the pictures. So what's the big deal? The artists not only use rich, vibrant colours but also gold foil and semi-precious stones for decoration!

The **Kalamkari paintings** of Andhra Pradesh too portray scenes from Hindu epics and mythology, but the artists use pen, cloth and natural dyes only. In fact, the word 'kalam' means pen and 'kari' is craftsmanship.

## for Paintings

## MUGHAL MINIATURES

**Miniature paintings** are tiny paintings on cloth, paper or palm leaves. This art developed in the 10th century, but it was under the Mughals that it flourished, blending Persian and Indian styles. The Mughal rulers wanted their deeds of valour and grand events at their court captured for all to admire. They even asked painters to accompany them to battle. So while war elephants trumpeted and arrows flew, the poor trembling artists painted on . . . !

*An exquisite Mughal miniature*

## MORE MINIATURE MAGIC

Like the Mughals, Hindu kings too encouraged various schools of miniature painting. The **Rajput paintings** portrayed scenes from the epics and the life of Lord Krishna. These works of art depicted animals, birds and people against lush landscapes. So did the **Pahari paintings** from the Himalayan regions, like those of the **Kangra** and **Garhwal** schools, all of which had Krishna as the central figure.

*A colourful Madhubani style painting*

## WATCH THAT WALL!

The **Mithila** or **Madhubani** style of painting is special to Bihar. The artists, mostly women, painted on almost anything—the mud walls of their homes, floors, vessels, and on special occasions, even elephants! They used only natural colours, grinding berries or crushing flowers to obtain some basic shades. So what did they paint with? Fingers, matchsticks, twigs . . . Today, Madhubani paintings are available on paper and cloth.

**Kamangari paintings** were once a speciality of Kutch and Kamangari artists too painted on walls. Most of them were Muslims but they readily painted scenes from the Hindu epics. When travellers described the strange new things they had seen, like trains and cricket matches, they painted those as well! Planning to get a Kamangari artist to jazz up your bedroom wall with pictures of your favourite cricket stars? Sorry, you're too late. By the 19th century, no one wanted the Kamangari paintings any more. So the art died out.

# for Palaces

If someone whisked you away to a magnificent building with turrets and towers, murals and marble staircases, grand furniture and gurgling fountains, where would you be? Probably, in a palace like one of the many in our country.

The Mysore Palace, where the famous Dussehra celebrations take place

## SOUTHERN SUPERSTAR

The maharajas, who once ruled various kingdoms in India, built colossal palaces. Mysore, in Karnataka, is often called the City of Palaces, because the place is dotted with them. The splendid **Mysore Palace** is the most famous of these. It is renowned for its spectacular celebrations during the Dussehra festival, when the city comes alive with dazzling processions and pageants, dance and music.

On Vijayadashami, the last day of the festival, which marks the triumph of good over evil, thousands arrive to watch the spectacular parade of richly decorated elephants and floats, which set off from the palace grounds. Nearly one lakh bulbs light up the palace during this festival!

The iconic landmark of Jaipur, the Hawa Mahal

## PALACE OF THE WINDS

**Hawa Mahal** may not be the grandest palace in Jaipur, but it certainly is the most unusual. It was built in 1799 by Maharaja Pratap Singh and designed by Lal Chand Ustad. This five-storeyed building in sandstone is shaped like the crown of Lord Krishna! With 953 tiny latticed windows, it resembles an intricate honeycomb. Through these, the royal ladies could peep out into the streets and watch the court processions and parades, without being seen.

The sprawling Umaid Bhawan Palace at Jodhpur

## HOME, HUGE HOME!

The **Umaid Bhawan Palace** in Jodhpur has an astonishing 347 rooms, and is one of the world's largest residences. Part of it has now been converted into a luxury hotel. Maharaja Umaid Singh started building it in 1929, to help his people by providing them with employment, when the kingdom was reeling under a famine. It took 5000 people some 15 years to complete the structure, and the money the workers earned helped them and their families to survive.

# for Palaces

*The grand Falaknuma Palace at Hyderabad*

## KERALA KALEIDOSCOPE

There are many interesting tales about the sprawling **Padmanabhapuram Palace** complex, which is about 50 km from Thiruvananthapuram, the capital of Kerala. It was built in the 17th century by the ruler of Travancore. The palace was carefully designed to keep the royal family safe. Weapons of various kinds were stored in recesses in the walls of many of the rooms. The palace also had a secret underground passage through which the king and his family could escape when danger loomed.

## MIRROR OF THE SKY

Do you know how the exquisite and grand **Falaknuma Palace** in Hyderabad got its name? 'Falaknuma' means mirror of the sky in Urdu. The palace, which is about 2000 feet above sea level, seems to reach up to the clouds and reflects the moods of the sky.

What else is special about the Falaknuma Palace? It was built in the shape of a scorpion! Besides, it has several priceless treasures, one of the best collections of Qurans in the country, and a large number of fabulous Venetian chandeliers. Each is crafted out of so many fiddly bits and pieces that the chandeliers take months to clean. The palace has a gigantic dining table, which is one of the largest in the world. Once upon a time, 101 guests sat around it and ate in style out of gold and silver plates!

*The impressive entrance to the Padmanabhapuram Palace*

## BIG SCREEN BONANAZA

Overlooking Lake Pichola in Udaipur is the largest palace complex in Rajasthan. It is the **City Palace**, built by Maharana Udai Singh in the 16th century. Four centuries later, some scenes from the James Bond movie, *Octopussy*, were shot there.

Several gates lead to the palace complex, with marble arches between them. On special occasions in the past, the Maharanas were weighed there with gold and silver. This wealth was then distributed among the public!

*The majestic City Palace at Udaipur*

# for Panchatantra

We have all read stories in which animals speak and act like human beings. When such a tale has a moral at the end or teaches us a lesson, it is called a fable. The world's best-loved fables, like the Panchatantra, come from India!

## LISTEN AND LEARN

Have you read the story of the merchant who borrowed an iron balance from his friend and then refused to return it, claiming that the rats had eaten it? Or the one about the heron who tricked and ate all the fish in his pond, and then had his neck wrung when he tried the same stunt on a crab? You'll find these tales and more in the earliest and most famous collection of fables in the world, our very own Panchatantra!

Around the 3rd century BCE, there was a wise king who had three dim-witted sons. So he asked an old teacher called **Vishnu Sharman** to teach the princes, and turn them into smart, able men.

Vishnu Sharman devised a clever way to make them learn. He began to narrate delightful stories in which animals behaved like people. Each story had a moral at the end, such as 'united we stand', 'silence is golden', and so on. By listening to the tales, the princes learnt how to conduct themselves wisely, judge people well, pick trustworthy friends, and solve problems of administration.

These stories were put together in five sections called the 'Panchatantra,' which means Five Principles. Over the years, it spread to Persia, Europe and South-East Asia, and was translated from Sanskrit into more than 50 languages, across the world.

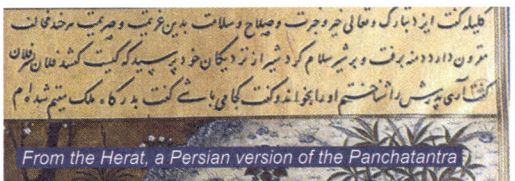

From the Herat, a Persian version of the Panchatantra

## THE MORE THE MERRIER!

Two other collections of similar fables appeared later, in India: **Hitopadesha**, which means good advice and the **Jataka tales**. The Jataka tales are said to be about the previous lives of Buddha, often in animal form. These tales, as well as the Hitopadesha, aim to encourage the young to lead good lives.

## for Ports

For thousands of years in the past, Indians were masters of the seas. They were actively engaged in trading with countries in Europe, Africa and Asia. In fact, ports both on the eastern and western coast of India were bustling hubs of the ancient sea routes linking all these continents.

## BYGONE BRAVEHEARTS

The Indian seafaring tradition probably dates back to the time of the Indus Valley Civilization. Some of the important Indus Valley ports were **Lothal**, **Dholavira**, **Bharuch** and **Khamba**t, in Gujarat.

The ancient port cities of the Chola, Pandya and Pallava dynasties of South India, such as **Kaveripoompattinam**, **Mahabalipuram** and **Arikamedu**, developed in course of time, as trade with distant lands flourished. The same was true of the Vijayanagar Empire, which is said to have had 300 ports!

## MIND YOUR TUSKS!

The Kutchi seafarers of Gujarat were particularly adventurous. Till a couple of centuries ago, **Mandvi** in Kutch was a major port with a thriving shipbuilding industry. Merchants would sail to Arabia and Africa with textiles, sugar, rice and oil and return with dates, timber and elephant tusks for the ivory carvers. The tusks were transported in bullock carts and were so huge that they either went crash-bang-bump against the houses lining the narrow streets, or got stuck in the windows, doorways and balconies!

## MAKE OR BREAK

Shipbuilding was one of the important industries in ancient India. In fact, the world's earliest known dockyard, where ships were loaded and unloaded, repaired and built was in the Indus Valley port of **Lothal** in Gujarat.

Now, **Alang** in Gujarat is notable for a different reason. It has the biggest ship-breaking yard in the world. It recycles nearly 30 per cent of the ships in the world, which have been scrapped.

*The archaeological remains of the town of Lothal*

## TRADERS, RAIDERS, CRUSADERS

Once the intrepid traveller **Vasco da Gama** discovered the sea route to India in 1498, the Portuguese, Dutch, English and French began to arrive in India to trade. Soon, missionaries from the West, like **St Francis Xavier**, also came along with the traders, to spread the message of Christianity.

The adventurers from the West soon began fighting each other and the local rulers for control of the ports, for that would put them in charge of the trade in spices and other goods. The British triumphed in the end and slowly started to take over the country as well. They developed many of the ports like **Calcutta** (Kolkata), **Bombay** (Mumbai), **Madras** (Chennai) and **Surat**.

*Chennai harbour in the 1890s*

## DID YOU KNOW?

India now has around 200 ports, of which 13 are major ones. The ports are vital for the country's economy as India's main exports (pharmaceutical products, iron and steel, garments, petroleum products and vehicles) and imports (crude oil, gold and silver, electronic goods and precious stones) are handled by them.

Of all the major ports in the country, **Kolkata** is the oldest, and **Mumbai** the biggest. **Nhava Sheva**, near Mumbai, was set up to relieve the congestion in Mumbai port. **Vishakhapatnam** is an important naval base, and India's first nuclear submarine was launched there. **Chennai** is the largest port on the eastern coast.

*Ships lining the Kolkata Port by night*

## TRICKS OF THE TRADE

**Madras** (Chennai) was an important port during the time of the British Raj. But as it does not have a natural harbour, ships had to anchor some miles at sea. The waters were rough, and travellers had to be brought ashore in country boats. When the passengers were midway to the shore, the smart cookies who rowed the boats would demand more money, or else . . .

**P** for Post

India has the largest number of post offices (over 1,55,000) and postal workers in the world. Once upon a time, people used pigeons to send messages, but we've come a long way since then. So how did it all happen?

## I SPY

When kings conquered new regions in order to build massive empires, they needed to find out what was happening in the distant parts of their kingdom. They also had to send instructions to the people they had left in charge. The Mauryas and, later, the Muslim invaders including the Mughals had relays of mail runners and horse or camel riders to carry their messages. These men also acted as spies for the king.

As the Mughal empire expanded, gathering news became really important. To speed up the delivery of mail, the Mughals built a vast network of excellent roads.

The Mughal Emperor Aurangzeb came up with a crafty plan to make sure no one dawdled on the way. Runners who were late were fined a quarter of their salary, but they too found ways of making up for this. Initially, the mail carriers carried only the royal mail. Soon, however, they quietly began accepting bribes from merchants to take their mail as well, on the sly.

## LUNCH IS SERVED!

The mail runners, in particular, had a difficult and dangerous job, as they were sometimes attacked by wild animals and bandits. All that they had to defend themselves was a pointed stick with bells, which they jingled all the way. During the time of the British Raj, the runners were accompanied by bandmasters or drummers to keep wild animals away!

Nowadays, mail is mostly transported by train, ship and aeroplane. However, animals and mail runners as well as bullock carts and bikes are still used in some places.

# for Post

## TALE OF THE FIRST AIR MAIL

In the early 1900s, the priest of the Holy Trinity Church in Allahabad wanted to raise money to build a hostel for Indian students. People were told that they could have their letters delivered by air for a fee of six annas (about 37 paise), which would be donated for the construction of the hostel. Some 6500 items of mail were collected, and in 1911, a French pilot called **Henri Pequet** carried them in a biplane from Allahabad to Naini. The journey covered 18 km in 27 minutes. It was the first Air Mail flight in the world, and it happened in India!

## GOODIES GALORE

Aeroplanes, bridges, birds, butterflies, animals, flowers, festivals, national leaders like Mahatma Gandhi, and cricket and films as well . . . we have postage stamps celebrating them all, and more! The stamps come in various shapes, sizes and forms. We even have stamps that smell of sandalwood!

But when did it all begin? In the mid-19th century, when the subcontinent was under British rule, India became the first country in Asia to issue postage stamps. The earliest stamps were released in Sindh, and were referred to as **Scinde Dawks**. Can you guess why? The British spelt Sindh as 'Scinde' and Dak, which means post in Hindi, as 'Dawk'!

The scenic village of Hikkim, where the world's highest post office is located

## POWER TO THE POST OFFICE!

• India has the highest post office in the world. It is located in **Hikkim**, Himachal Pradesh, at a height of 4440 m.

• There is a floating post office on the **Dal Lake** in Kashmir.

• In 1988, India set up a post office in Antarctica at the Indian base there, called **Dakshin Gangotri**.

• Indian post offices not only deliver mail and transfer money, but also provide services like life insurance and pension plans. They have various savings schemes, which are particularly helpful to people in faraway places where there are no banks.

## for Queens

Turn the pages of Indian history, and you will surely find several extraordinary women who sacrificed everything to protect the freedom of their land and their people, such as these wise and valiant queens who ruled our country long ago . . .

### FEARLESS FIREBRAND

**Rani Laxmibai (1835–1858)**
She was one of the most heroic leaders in the Uprising of 1857 against British rule. When her husband, the Raja of Jhansi, died, the British refused to recognize their adopted son Damodar Rao as the heir to the throne and decided to take over the kingdom.

'I will NEVER surrender Jhansi!' vowed Rani Laxmibai, joining the rebellion. As a young girl, she had learnt to ride, shoot and fight. So dressed like a man, she led her troops in battle. Eventually, she died fighting bravely against the British.

Did you know that the Rani's cannons had been given rousing names like Kadak Bijli (Thunder and Lightning)? Some of them were also operated by women.

OH ... CANONS! *SO SORRY!* I THOUGHT THEY WERE BOLLYWOOD ITEM NUMBERS!

**Other great queens who fought the British:** Begum Hazrat Mahal of Oudh, Rani Avantibai of Ramgarh and Rani Chennamma of Kittur.

### FEISTY FIGHTER

**Razia Sultan (1205–1240)**
Since her childhood little Razia had sat beside her father, Sultan Iltutmish, the ruler of Delhi, when he discussed matters of government and planned his strategy for war. Later, Iltutmish appointed Razia his heir although no sultan had ever made a woman his successor! The nobles, however, refused to accept her and crowned her brother the sultan. But he turned out to be a flop and Razia was back again on the throne.

At a time when women were mostly confined within the home, Razia rode into battle on an elephant, dressed like a soldier. In the few years that she ruled before she was dethroned by her enemies, she was much loved by her people.

Did you know that Razia was India's first female sultan?

**Muslim queens who were the power behind the throne:** Chand Bibi of Ahmadnagar and Mughal Empress Noor Jahan.

The valiant Rani Laxmibai

## for Queens

# WISE WARRIOR

## Ahilyabai Holkar (1725 – 1795)

After the death of her husband and, later, of her father-in-law, Ahilyabai Holkar became the ruler of Malwa. Though some nobles mumbled and grumbled about this because she was a woman, the army which she had led in battle, supported her enthusiastically. And so did her people for she proved to be an able sovereign whose charity was legendary. She used her own funds to build temples, roads, wells, tanks and rest houses not only in Malwa, but also in pilgrimage centres from the Himalayas all the way to South India.

Did you know that Ahilyabai Holkar was called the philosopher-queen?

**Other benevolent rulers**: Rani Mangammal of Madurai, Rani Rudramma Devi of Warrangal and Maharani Gowri Lakshmibayi of Travancore.

# FREEDOM OR DEATH!

## Rani Abbakka Chowta (1525–1570?)

In the 16th century, the Portuguese were trying to capture the ports on the western coast of India to control the spice trade. One of them was Ullal near Mangalore, the capital of Rani Abbakka. The Portuguese, who had better arms and trained warriors, were confident of victory. But Abbakka came up with a smart plan. Under her instructions, a small band of fishermen sailed stealthily towards the Portuguese warships and threw hundreds of burning coconut torches at them. Several ships were sunk, leaving a trail of death and destruction.

Time and again, Rani Abbakka fought and pushed back the Portuguese, until she was betrayed and captured. But even in prison she rebelled and died fighting like a true patriot.

Did you know that Abbakka was called Rani Abhaya (Fearless Queen)? She was probably the earliest woman freedom fighter in the country to challenge a western power.

**Other early freedom fighters**: Both Rani Durgavati of Gondwana and Chennamma of Keladi fought against the Mughals.

*Ahilya Ghat by River Ganga at Varanasi was built by the wise queen, Ahilyabai Holkar.*

# for Qutub Minar

Which monument has 379 steps, stands about 72.5 m high, and is the tallest stone tower in India? Yes, it is the magnificent and towering Qutub Minar!

## WHY, WHAT AND WHEN

To celebrate his triumph in battle against the Rajputs, the Turkish invader **Qutb-ud-din Aibak** began constructing the Qutub Minar in 1193 CE, as a victory tower, and as a minaret from where Muslims could be called to their prayers. This imposing sandstone structure with carvings and verses from the Quran stands on the outskirts of present-day Delhi. Its construction was completed by his successor **Iltutmish**.

The tower is surrounded by many other structures and the entire area is called the Qutub complex. This has been declared a UNESCO World Heritage Site.

### ISN'T THAT STRANGE?

• The Qutub Minar was struck by lightning twice.

• The minar does not stand straight, but leans to one side.

• Some historians say that the construction of the tower was started by the Rajput ruler Prithviraj, so that his daughter could gaze upon the holy River Yamuna before saying her prayers. But he was defeated by the Turks in battle. Once Qutb-ud-din took over Delhi, he continued to build the minar with a totally different goal in mind. From the top of the Qutub Minar, his successors would be able to keep watch over the movements of the fierce Mongol hordes that threatened Delhi.

## METAL MARVEL

The **Quwwat-ul-Islam Mosque** in the Qutub complex is the earliest mosque built by the Delhi sultans. According to the inscriptions there, its core was constructed using materials from 27 temples demolished by the invaders.

In the courtyard of the ancient mosque is the far-famed **Iron Pillar**. So what's the big deal about it? The pillar is believed to have been erected by **King Vikramaditya** and has stood in the open for 1600 years without rusting!

The Qutub Minar was built as a victory tower.

# for Railways

India's vast rail network, the Indian Railways, links every part of the country, from mountains to metros, and hill resorts to holy towns.

## HOW IT ALL BEGAN

On 16 April 1853, the first train on the Indian subcontinent huffed and puffed from Bori Bunder in Bombay (now Mumbai) to Thane, a distance of 33 km. The coaches were pulled by a shiny new engine called the Falkland. With that the **Great Indian Peninsular Railway** (GIP) opened its operations.

By the time India gained its independence in 1947, there were 42 different railway systems spread across the country. In 1951, they were all taken over by the Government of India and turned into one big organization called the **Indian Railways**. This has now become one of the largest rail networks in the world with over 68,000 km of track, and carries more than 23 million passengers every day!

## BACKTRACKING

The **National Railway Museum** at Chanakyapuri, New Delhi, has a wonderful collection of antique steam locomotives, carriages, saloons and other railway artefacts. The prize exhibit is the world's oldest operational steam locomotive, the *Fairy Queen*, built in 1855. On some days, another one of the exhibits, the old *Patiala State Steam Monorail*, is steamed up and runs on its track around the museum!

## THANK GOODNESS FOR THE GOODS

Most of the revenue earned by the Indian Railways comes from transporting freight such as coal, cement, petroleum products, fertilizers, sugar, jute, tea, textiles, automobiles, agricultural produce, and iron and steel, throughout the country.

*Bholu, the guard elephant and mascot of the Indian Railways*

## FUN FACTS

• The mascot of the Indian Railways is **Bholu** the guard elephant.

• The railway platform at **Gorakhpur**, at 1366 m, is the longest in the world.

• The station with the shortest name is **Ib** in Orissa.

• The station with the longest name is **Sri Venkatanarasimharajuvariapeta** in Tamil Nadu.

# for Railways

*An old-style steam engine*

## FAST AND FAMOUS

The Indian Railways played a huge role in speeding up the country's economic, social, industrial and agricultural development, and also helped to bring people from different places closer together. Let's take a look at some of the trains run by the Indian Railways.

## A ROYAL DELIGHT

If you want to be treated like royalty, get on board one of the luxury trains in India. The most famous of these is the *Royal Rajasthan on Wheels*, which offers you a 'Week in Wonderland'. Sink back in splendour and explore the magic of palaces and forts, wildlife parks and historical monuments along the way.

*Inside the palatial* Royal Rajasthan on Wheels

## METRO MAGIC

Growing cities, an expanding population, overcrowded buses and traffic jams! People were almost screaming for an easier way to travel within cities, and the government came up with the **Mass Rapid Transit System** (MRTS). The metro rail projects are a part of this, the first one being the Kolkata Metro, established in 1984. The rapidly expanding Delhi Metro network is the biggest, and Bengaluru has just made a beginning. Similar projects are also being planned for many other cities like Hyderabad, Nagpur and Ahmedabad.

## TRAVEL ANYWHERE

• While the most common trains are the express, mail and passenger trains, the Indian Railways runs a few special trains too.

• The **Rajdhani** trains are fast passenger trains that connect several cities to the capital, New Delhi. The **Duronto Express** trains are the fastest long-distance trains of the Indian Railways.

• The **Shatabdi Express** trains are inter-city express trains. The Grand Trunk Express or GT started running in 1929, from Peshawar to Mangalore, and that was one of the longest train routes. It now runs between Delhi and Chennai.

• 'Classless' or single-class trains with lower fares, such as the **Janata Express**, **Jansewa Express** and **Garib Rath** trains, have also been introduced.

• The **Lifeline Express** trains are hospital trains, which visit different parts of the country, especially villages, where there are no doctors or medical services. They provide medical care to the local people.

# for Rajasaurus

REX, DID YOU READ THE NEWS? OUR COUSIN RAJA HAS BEEN FOUND IN INDIA.

## OUR VERY OWN DINO

We know that dinosaurs lived in India because their fossil remains, like their eggs and bones, have been found here. What is our most exciting dino discovery so far? In 1983, the fossilized bones of a huge dinosaur, unknown till then, were excavated in the Narmada River Valley! The dino was later named Rajasaurus. To find out what the Rajasaurus looked like, a detailed map was made of the position where its bones were found. Then, the bones were coloured with a marker. And abracadabra . . . the partial skeleton of a meat-eating dinosaur emerged, giving enough clues to create a model of this reptile.

The Rajasaurus became extinct 65 million years ago. Scientists believe that huge meteors crashed into the earth, and this led to climatic changes that killed all the dinosaurs. Where can you see the Rajasaurus now? The **Indroda Dinosaur and Fossil Park** in Gujarat has a huge model of it, as well as models of other dinosaurs, fossils of dinosaur skeletons, casts of footprints and the world's second largest collection of dinosaur eggs.

## FUN FACTS

• **Full name**: *Rajasaurus narmadensis* (which means regal lizard from the Narmada region)

• **Where it was found**: Gujarat and Madhya Pradesh, in the Narmada River valley

• **Lived**: 65–70 million years ago, in India

• **Size**: 9 m long

• **Diet**: Meat, including other dinosaurs

• **Special features**: Unusual head crest or horn

India's very own dinosaur, the Rajasaurus narmadensis

## for Rangoli

The rangoli is a symbol of auspiciousness. It is part of the Indian tradition and a popular art form that is passed on from generation to generation.

## KNOW YOUR RANGOLI

The word 'rangoli' comes from the Sanskrit words 'rang' (colour) and 'aavali' (lines). A rangoli is a pattern made with lines of colour on the floor, on walls, and even in the street.

**People believe that the rangoli:**

• Provides a colourful welcome to visitors (including gods and goddesses, especially during festivals).

• Is also an offering of food for ants and birds. This is why the traditional rangoli is created with natural colours and rice flour.

• Keeps evil spirits away . . . provided there are no gaps in the rangoli through which they can slip in!

DON'T FORGET! A RANGOLI A DAY KEEPS THE SPIRITS AWAY!

## THE FIRST RANGOLI

There is a legend that in an ancient kingdom, there was a wise head priest who was much loved by all. When his son died, the whole kingdom was plunged into grief. So Brahma the Creator told the priest to make a picture of the boy. When this was done, Brahma breathed into it and brought the boy back to life. That is said to be the first rangoli!

WONDER WHO *THIS* RANGOLI IS!

## COLOURFUL FACTS

• A rangoli could be a geometric pattern, a picture of a god or a goddess, like Ganesha or Lakshmi, the sun and moon, animals, flowers, birds and lamps. It could also depict a scene from history or mythology.

• The rangoli is known by various names in different parts of the country, such as, **alpana** in Bengal, **aripana** in Bihar, **kolam** in Kerala and Tamil Nadu, and **rangoli** in Karnataka, Gujarat and Maharashtra.

• Did you know that rangolis are made with rice flour, pastes and powders, flowers and even sand and paint? Nowadays, plastic sticker rangolis are available too!

# for Religion

**Did you know that four major religions—Hinduism, Buddhism, Jainism and Sikhism—began in India, and people of many faiths live together here in harmony? Approximately 79 per cent of Indians are Hindus. But the Constitution of India grants everyone the freedom to follow any religion. Besides, all religions are treated as equal.**

## THE MAJOR RELIGIONS OF INDIA

### HINDUISM
This is the oldest religion in the world and goes back more than 4000 years. A seal found in the ancient city of Mohenjodaro of a seated male figure surrounded by animals is believed to be **Pashupati**, an early version of **Lord Shiva**. Unlike most religions, Hinduism was not started by a single person.

### HINDUS BELIEVE THAT

• There is a Supreme God, who can be worshipped in various forms, such as Shiva, Vishnu, Durga, etc.

• God is in everything, so we must respect and care for all—men, women, animals, trees, rivers and so on.

• Whatever we do, good or bad, has a matching effect. This is called karma and our actions shape and control it.

• We are reborn after we die, and each life depends on the way we've lived our earlier life.

**HOLY CITIES**: Badrinath, Kedarnath, Varanasi, Tirupathi, Rameswaram

**SACRED BOOKS**: The Vedas, the Puranas, the Bhagavad Gita, and the epics—Ramayana and Mahabharata

**MAJOR FESTIVALS**: Diwali, Holi, Navaratri

A Chola bronze of Lord Shiva as Nataraja

### ISLAM
**Prophet Muhammad** founded Islam in 610 CE in Arabia. His followers are called Muslims. Arab traders and Muslim invaders brought Islam to India. Now, the Muslim population in the country is the third largest in the world.

### MUSLIMS BELIEVE THAT

• There is one God.

• God revealed the Quran to Prophet Muhammad so that he could teach people the truth.

• Muslims should pray five times a day, donate to charity, fast during Ramadan, and go on a pilgrimage to Mecca.

**HOLY CITIES**: Mecca in Saudi Arabia, Jerusalem in Israel (which is a holy city for Christians and Jews as well)

**SACRED BOOK**: Quran

**HOLY DAYS**: Muharram, Ramadan, Eid al-Fitr

# for Religion

## BUDDHISM

**Gautama Buddha** (Prince Siddhartha), who gave up his kingdom to seek the Truth, founded Buddhism around 525 BCE.

### BUDDHISTS BELIEVE THAT

• We should not kill, steal, lie or harm any living beings.

• We will be reborn after we die and what we do in this life will affect our next life.

• Prayer and good deeds will free us from this cycle of birth and death and bring us real happiness.

**HOLY CITIES**: Bodh Gaya, Sarnath, Lumbini (Buddha's birthplace in Nepal)

**SACRED BOOKS**: The Sutras and the Tripitaka (Three Baskets)

**MAJOR FESTIVALS**: Vesak (Buddha's birthday), Buddhist New Year

*A statue of the Buddha at Bodh Gaya*

## JAINISM

**Vardhamana Mahavira** founded Jainism in the 6th century BCE.

### JAINS BELIEVE THAT

• All forms of life are equally important. So we must follow the path of ahimsa (non-violence) and not hurt any living beings, even insects.

• We can free ourselves from the cycle of birth, death and suffering through right belief, right knowledge and right action.

**HOLY CITIES**: Shravanabelagola (Karnataka), where there is a colossal 10th century statue of the Jain saint Bahubali, and Mount Abu (Rajasthan)

**SACRED BOOKS**: Karmaprabhrta and Kasayaprabhrta, and writings based upon the teachings of Mahavira

**MAJOR FESTIVAL**: Mahavira's birthday

## SIKHISM

**Guru Nanak** founded Sikhism in Punjab in the 16th century.

### SIKHS BELIEVE THAT

• There is one God who creates and protects us, and everyone is equal before him.

• We should be honest, work hard, serve others, and lead a good life.

• The five symbols of the religion should be worn by Sikh men. They are: kacha (underpants), kanga (comb), kirpan (sword), kada (steel bangle) and kesh (long hair).

**HOLY CITY**: Amritsar where the sacred Harmandir Sahib (Golden Temple) stands

**SACRED BOOK**: Guru Granth Sahib

**MAJOR FESTIVALS**: Baisakhi (New Year's Day), Diwali, Guru Nanak's birthday

# for Religion

A stained-glass painting of Jesus Christ

## CHRISTIANITY

**Jesus Christ** founded Christianity over 2000 years ago, in what is now Israel. St Thomas, who came to Malabar (Kerala) in 52 CE, St Francis Xavier, who landed in India in 1542, and later, the Portuguese, French and British who conquered India, helped spread the religion in the country.

## CHRISTIANS BELIEVE THAT

• There is one God.

• God sent his son, Jesus Christ, to earth to teach people to love, help and forgive one another.

• Jesus gave his life to save the human race, but was later resurrected (raised from the dead).

**SACRED BOOK**: The Bible

**MAJOR FESTIVALS**: Easter, Christmas

## OTHER RELIGIONS

Many who were persecuted in their own country because of their religion found refuge in India.

**ZOROASTRIANISM** was founded by Zoroaster who was born around 628 BCE in Persia (now Iran). Zoroastrians worship **Ahura Mazda**, and revere fire as his symbol. When Persia fell to Muslim invaders, the Zoroastrians were persecuted, and in the 6th and 7th centuries, many of them fled to India where they came to be known as Parsis.

In the 19th century, a Persian called **Baha'u'llah** founded the **BAHA'I** religion. The Baha'is believe that all religions are pathways to God, who reveals the truth to people through the teachings of prophets like Abraham, Buddha, Zoroaster, Jesus and Muhammad. The Baha'is too were persecuted in Persia and many fled to India. In fact, the largest number of Zoroastrians and Baha'is in the world today live in India.

There are small communities of Jews as well in India. They follow **JUDAISM**, which, like Christianity and Islam, originated in Israel. Jews believe that there is one God who has created us and we should follow his laws. The Jews arrived in India 2500 years ago. Their oldest synagogue (their place of worship) is in Cochin, Kerala.

The magnificent Lotus Temple of the Baha'is in Delhi

# for Rupee

**What do India, Bhutan, Pakistan, Sri Lanka, Nepal, Mauritius, and the Maldives have in common? Their currency is called the rupee. And the name 'rupee' comes from the Sanskrit word 'rupya', which means silver.**

## RUPEE ROUND-UP

Metal coins were being made in India way back in 600 BCE. But it was the Afghan conqueror **Sher Shah Suri** who introduced the first silver coin called the 'rupiya' in 1540 CE. It was in 1835 that the British East India Company, which controlled much of India at the time, brought out a standard silver rupee. Before that, each state had its own kind of rupee or rupiya.

Coins and notes were issued with portraits of British rulers, until India became a free country in 1947. After Independence, these were replaced by Asoka's Lion Capital at Sarnath. In 1957, India switched to the decimal system, and the rupee was divided into 100 naye paise or new paise (which later became just 'paise'). Earlier, the rupee had been divided into 16 annas and each anna was divided into 12 pice.

After a nationwide contest, a new rupee symbol was adopted in 2010. It is the Devanagari letter र (Ra) with an extra bar. The two lines look like an equal sign . . . to show that the nation is striving for economic equality for all.

## ANIMAL ANTICS

Many ancient coins were stamped with pictures of animals like elephants, lions and bulls. Those stamped with the boar (*varaha* in Sanskrit) were also called varaha!

## DID YOU KNOW?

The value of every note is inscribed in 17 Indian languages, including Hindi and English! The **Reserve Bank of India** (RBI) manages the country's currency and the government issues India's banknotes. These are printed at special presses in Nasik, Dewas, Mysore and Hoshangabad. Our coins are minted at the Government of India mints in Mumbai, Kolkata, Hyderabad and Noida.

# for Saints

India is often called the land of saints. So who were the saints? They were holy men and women driven by bhakti or a deep love of God. They spent their lives helping others because they saw God everywhere and in everything.

## LOVE CONQUERS ALL

Through the ages, saints have spread the message that we must love all living beings. Caste and class are unimportant, and everyone is equal in the eyes of God. Some of the celebrated saints in Tamil Nadu were the **Alvars**, who were immersed in the worship of Vishnu; and the **Nayanmars**, who wandered from place to place singing the praises of Shiva. Then, there were the **Haridasas** of Karnataka, who were devotees of Krishna. The most illustrious of these were Purandaradasa and Kanakadasa.

Among the saints were kings and scholars as well as potters, cowherds, cobblers, fishermen, hunters and even the so-called 'untouchables'. They composed hundreds of songs in praise of God, and some of them also performed miracles.

LIKE WE SAY IN TENNIS, *LOVE ALL!*

*Kanakadasa singing in praise of Lord Krishna*

## MOVING MIRACLES

Legend says that **Kanakadasa** was not allowed inside the temple of Krishna at Udipi because he belonged to a lower caste. So Kanaka stood outside the temple and began to sing in praise of the lord. Suddenly, a small opening appeared in the wall, and the deity bent towards Kanaka so that he could get a good view! Even today, it remains in this position.

Similarly, the 'untouchable' saint **Nandanar** was not permitted to enter the Shiva temple at Tirupungur (Tamil Nadu). All he wanted was a glimpse of the lord, but the huge stone Nandi (bull) in front of Shiva, blocked his view. Praying fervently, Nandanar just stood outside . . . and then, the Nandi moved so that the devotee could see the deity!

# for Saints

The prominent saints from the northern part of the country were **Surdas**, **Tulsidas**, **Meera Bai**, **Jnaneswar**, **Namdeo**, **Eknath**, **Kabir** and **Tukaram**. There were also great Sufi saints like **Nizamuddin Auliya**, who attracted both Hindu and Muslim followers.

## GOD KNOWS NO CASTE

**Tukaram**, a popular saint of Maharashtra, spent his life writing and singing about God. Some people were angry with Tukaram for daring to write about God, for he belonged to a lower caste. So they forced him to throw the palm leaves on which he had written his songs into the river. Tukaram was heartbroken. For 13 days, without food or water, he sat praying. Suddenly, all the palm leaves floated to the surface, undamaged by the water! Many of Tukaram's enemies then realized what a great soul he was.

Sant Tukaram

## WOMEN SAINTS AND THEIR MANY WONDERS

There were great women saints too like **Andal** (Tamil Nadu), **Lalleshwari** or **Lal Ded** (Kashmir) and **Akka Mahadevi** (Karnataka). But the most famous of them all was **Meera**, a Rajput princess, who was so deeply devoted to Krishna that she spent all her life singing of his glory. Her husband's family was outraged. They tried to poison her, but the poison changed to nectar. Then they sent her a cobra in a basket, but it turned into a garland. She later joined a band of devotees going to the temple of Krishna at Dwaraka, and there, as a flash of light, she merged into the deity.

Akka Mahadevi

## SINGING GOD'S GLORY

**Kabir** was a weaver who composed songs as he worked. He taught that people should seek God not in temples or in mosques but in their hearts. Kabir had both Hindu and Muslim disciples, and after his death they began to argue over his last rites. However, when they lifted the cloth covering his body, they found only a heap of flowers. The Muslims buried half the blossoms, and the Hindus cremated the other half. Kabir's couplets are so meaningful that they are recited even today.

## for Sari

**Across the subcontinent, it has been the traditional dress of women for over 5000 years. It comes in all colours of the rainbow and in hundreds of designs with motifs like flowers, animals, mangoes, peacocks, and so on. Yes, it's the sari!**

## FIGHTING FIT

The sari is a strip of cloth, usually six yards long and without a single stitch on it. Pleat and tuck it at the waist, then drape one end over the shoulder, make sure you have a matching choli, and you're done! Do you know why the sari and dhoti (a similar garment worn by men) are not stitched? Hindus used to once believe that any cloth pierced with a needle was impure.

Saris come in all sorts of fabrics like cotton, silk, organza, chiffon and polyester. They are worn in different styles as well. For instance, in certain communities in Tamil Nadu and Maharashtra, the traditional sari is nine yards long. Believe it or not, it is tucked between the legs in such a way that women can—and did—play tennis and even go for a swim in their saris! In fact, Rani Chennamma, the queen of Kittur, rode into battle against the enemy with her sari tucked in a similar style called the **veeragacche** or soldier's tuck.

## SARI WITH A STORY

Different regions in India have their own unique designs and fabrics. Some of the popular saris are: **Bandhani**, **Patola**, and **Paithani** in western India; **Banaras silk**, **Chanderi** and **Tanchoi** in the north; the splendid **Kanjeevaram** and **Mysore silks** in the south; and **Baluchari**, **Tanta** and **Jamdani** saris in the east.

The Baluchari saris of West Bengal are special because their borders portray stories from the Ramayana and the Mahabharata.

## OLD IS GOLD

In many rural areas, old saris are cleverly recycled into quilts, bags, dusters, towels and diapers. They are even used as hammocks for babies!

# S for Seven Sisters

**Rugged mountains and thundering rivers, lush green jungles teeming with wildlife, where few people choose to venture ... Is it any wonder that the Seven Sister States in the north-eastern corner of India are known as Paradise Unexplored?**

## SISTER ACT

Looking for adventure? Then head for the Seven Sisters of the North-Eastern Region or NER: **Arunachal Pradesh**, **Assam**, **Manipur**, **Meghalaya**, **Mizoram**, **Nagaland** and **Tripura**. **Sikkim**, the newest addition, became the eighth state in 2002. The Seven Sister States are home to more than 150 tribes that follow age-old customs and traditions. Fairs and festivals, song and dance are a part of their life. When it comes to food, they have some very unusual delicacies, such as roasted rats, worms, snakes and spiders! Want some?

*A tribal woman from Arunachal Pradesh*

*A traditional tribal dance from the North-East of India*

## FACT FILE

**Neighbouring Countries**: Myanmar, China, Bhutan and Bangladesh

**Neighbouring State**: West Bengal. Asom, known as the Gateway of the North-East, connects the Seven Sisters to the rest of India through a narrow strip of land called the Siliguri Corridor.

**Superstars**: The numerous national parks and wildlife sanctuaries, teeming with a huge variety of animals, birds and plants.

**Industries and Occupations**: These are linked to the tea plantations and oil and natural gas found in the region. The North-East is also known for its exquisite silks, jewellery, toys, pottery, and various handicrafts made of bamboo, cane and wood.

**Trouble in Paradise**: The people of the region feel that the Government of India has neglected them and not done enough to develop the region. Also, in many areas, hordes of immigrants from Bangladesh have taken over their lands and reduced them to a minority in their own homeland. This too has gone unchecked. So several groups in the North-East have been carrying on an armed struggle to break away from India and create independent nations.

# S for Seven Sisters

## DAZZLING AND DIFFERENT

The Seven Sisters are unlike any other region in India. So what makes them special?

### ARUNACHAL PRADESH

**The name means**: Land of the Dawn Lit Mountains
**Capital**: Itanagar

**That's Amazing!**
• The 400-year-old Buddhist monastery at **Tawang**, in Arunachal Pradesh, is one of the biggest monasteries in the country.

• Over 600 species of orchids are found in Arunachal Pradesh, making it the orchid paradise of India.

A one-horned rhino at the Kaziranga National Park in Asom.

### ASSAM

**The name means**: unequalled or unrivalled
**Capital:** Dispur

**That's Amazing!**
• Assam's **Kaziranga National Park** is home to many endangered animals like elephants, tigers and the one-horned rhino.

• **Majuli** in River Brahmaputra is the largest river island in India.

• The British first set up tea plantations in Assam way back in 1820. Today, Assam and West Bengal together produce 74 per cent of the tea grown in India.

Stone structures similar to Stonehenge can be found at Willong Khullen, a village in Manipur.

### MANIPUR

**The name means**: Jewelled Land
**Capital**: Imphal

**That's Amazing!**
• Manipur's **Keibul Lamjao National Park** is the only floating national park in India.

• The game of **polo** began in Manipur. It was a big hit with the British. Gradually, it grew to become an international sport, which is popular even today.

• The name of the state has its origin in a myth about the gods dancing. The story goes that Krishna and Radha were floating on the clouds and suddenly felt like dancing. So they came down to earth to a place surrounded by mountains and performed a graceful dance. Lord Shiva, who was watching them, was so impressed by their movements that he scattered precious gems to illumine the place where Radha and Krishna were dancing. That very same place is called Manipur today!

# S for Seven Sisters

Shillong, the capital of Meghalaya, as seen from Shillong Peak

## MEGHALAYA
**The name means**: Abode of the Clouds
**Capital**: Shillong

**That's Amazing!**
• **Mawsynram** and **Cherrapunjee**, the wettest places on earth, are in Meghalaya.

• Some of the longest caves in South Asia are found in the **Khasi Hills** there.

• Besides Kerala, Meghalaya is one of the few places in the world with a matrilineal system, under which the land and property is inherited and owned by women.

## MIZORAM
**The name means**: Land of the Hill People
**Capital**: Aizawl

**That's Amazing!**
• The people of Mizoram follow a code of behaviour known as **tlawmngaihna**. It means everyone should be unselfish, kind and helpful to one another.

• Once in 50 years, the bamboo blooms in Mizoram. These flowers attract thousands of rats, which invade the fields, gobble up all the crops, and cause a famine.

• While all of the North-East is known for the bamboo dance, it rightfully belongs to Mizoram. The **cheraw**, which gets its name from the Mizo word for bamboo, has been recognized as the oldest dance form in Mizoram.

## NAGALAND
**The name means**: Land of the Nagas
**Capital**: Kohima

**That's Amazing!**
• The Nagas were fierce warriors and headhunters too, once upon a time!

• They love to dance and their dances are named after animals, birds or insects, like the fly dance or the bear dance.

• The **Catholic Cathedral** at **Aradura Hill** is one of the largest cathedrals in the North-East. It houses the biggest wooden cross in the country.

## SIKKIM
**The name comes from**: a combination of two Limbu words: *Su*, meaning 'new', and *Khyim*, meaning 'palace', referring to the palace built by the state's first ruler
**Capital**: Gangtok

**That's Amazing!**
• It is India's least populous state, with a population of about six lakh people, so here's where you should go if you want to be far from the madding crowd!

• Sikkim is home to the magnificent **Kangchenjunga**, the highest peak in India and third highest in the world, and the high-altitude, biodiversity-rich **Khangchendzonga National Park**.

## TRIPURA
**The name comes from**: Goddess Tripurasundari, who is worshipped there
**Capital**: Agartala

**That's Amazing!**
• The **Neer Mahal** in Lake Rudrasagar near Agartala is a fantastic water palace with towers, turrets and moats.

• At the ancient pilgrimage centre of **Unakoti**, several spectacular images of Shiva and Ganesha have been sculpted on the hills. Legend has it that an inspired sculptor, who wanted to accompany Shiva and Parvati on their journey to Kailash, agreed to carve one crore images of the gods in a single day. But he managed to make only 99,99,999 images, hence the name Unakoti or one less than a crore!

## for Spice

India was known as the land of spices some 7000 years ago, drawing early seafarers like the Phoenicians and Arabs to these shores. It was the beginning of a long story of trade and conquest, which brought the subcontinent under western rule!

## WHY IS SPICE NICE?

Spices make our food smell good and taste oh-so-yummy. Also, before the days of refrigeration, spices helped to preserve food. Otherwise, people would have starved during the lean season.

The Portuguese navigator Vasco da Gama was the first to find a sea route from Europe to India. Although only two of the four ships he had set out with returned home safe, the cargo of spices he took back with him was worth 60 times what he had spent on making the voyage. The Portuguese were followed by the English, French and Dutch, and for centuries, they all fought fiercely for control of the spice trade. In the end, this led to the conquest of India by European powers.

## SPICY BUT PRICEY

In the West, spices were in great demand many centuries ago. Of course, they were very expensive, because they had to be brought all the way from Asia. Half a kilo of ginger cost as much as a sheep, and a sack of pepper was worth a man's life! Every year, Europe imported 2000 tonnes of spices. What they paid for this would have bought enough food grains to feed 15,00,000 people for a year! With the invention of refrigeration in the 19th century, the demand for spices declined, and their prices fell.

## FUNKY FACT

• India produces about 85 per cent of the spices in the world. The popular ones are: **pepper**, **chilli**, **turmeric**, **ginger**, **coriander**, **cardamom** and **cumin**. The fragrant **saffron** is the most expensive spice in the world.

*Indian spices brought Vasco da Gama to the coast of India in 1498.*

## for Sundarbans

**Can you name a place which is the largest mangrove forest in the world, a national park, a tiger reserve, and a UNESCO World Heritage Site all rolled into one? It is the Sundarbans, home to several species of animals, birds, reptiles and plants.**

The Sundarbans is criss-crossed with several river channels and creeks.

## MANGROVE MARVEL

The name 'Sundarbans' most probably comes from the Sundari trees found in the place. It also means beautiful jungle in Bengali. The Sundarbans covers 10,000 sq km in West Bengal and Bangladesh. It stretches along the **Bay of Bengal** in the slushy, swampy delta of the **Ganga**, **Brahmaputra** and **Meghna** rivers.

Why is the Sundarbans special? It not only has the largest mangrove forest in the world, but the only one where tigers prowl. Besides, it acts as a storm barrier and protects Kolkata and surrounding places from being flooded when cyclones strike.

WELCOME! I HOPE YOU HAVE BROUGHT ALONG ALL THOSE RELATIVES YOU DON'T LIKE TOO MUCH. WE'RE PLANNING A PARTY AND WILL NEED SNACKS.

## STOP, TRESPASSERS WILL BE EATEN!

The Sundarbans is home to hundreds of species of plants, animals, birds and reptiles. These include endangered species, such as the **Royal Bengal Tiger**, **wild boar**, **python**, **cobra**, **viper**, **crocodile**, **Gangetic Dolphin** and **monitor lizard**. Turtles like the **Olive ridleys** come here to nest.

The tigers in the Sundarbans are expert swimmers. Unlike most tigers, they swim long distances, and sometimes feed on fish and crabs. They are said to be man-eaters too. And they've got competition! The huge saltwater crocodiles in the Sundarbans—some of them are 22 feet long—also love snacking on humans.

In spite of these dangers, people still sneak into the forest in search of firewood and honey as it is often their only livelihood. The gypsies in the area train otters to work for them. The otters catch fish and also help them in poaching dolphins, by acting as decoys to lure them!

# for Taj Mahal

**The 17th century Mughal Emperor Shah Jahan built this magnificent monument in memory of his favourite wife, Mumtaz Mahal. It was considered one of the Wonders of the Medieval World, and is now a UNESCO World Heritage Site.**

## MARBLE MARVEL

The Taj, which was designed by **Ustad Ahmad Lahawri**, stands on the bank of River Yamuna in Agra. So what is the secret behind its splendour? Well, Shah Jahan spent 22 years building this colossal complex with its elegant domes and minarets, gardens and mosques, lotus pool and tomb.

More than 20,000 masons and craftsmen were employed to build the Taj Mahal and thousands of elephants, bullocks, camels and wagons transported the materials used in the construction. The glowing white marble for the main structure was brought from Makrana in Rajasthan. Huge quantities of precious and semi-precious stones were used for the engravings. These gems came from Tibet, Afghanistan, Sri Lanka, Central Asia, Persia, China and India.

## QUICK FIX

Before building the Taj Mahal, the masons had to make a gigantic scaffolding from which they could work. This was a kind of frame that was just like the Taj but made of bricks. Once the Taj was completed, Emperor Shah Jahan was informed that the scaffolding would take months to pull down. 'I want it done NOW, never mind the cost!' declared the impatient emperor. 'Whoever removes the bricks from the scaffolding can keep them.' In a jiffy, the poor people in the neighbourhood dismantled the structure, and happily carted away the bricks to build their own homes!

## FROM PALACE TO PRISON

Shah Jahan's son Aurangzeb seized the throne in 1658 and imprisoned his father at the Agra Fort. It is said that Shah Jahan spent his last days gazing at the Taj Mahal from his window. When he died, he was buried in the Taj, next to his wife.

The magnificent Taj Mahal and the mosque of red sandstone nearby.

## for Temples

Mandir. Kovil. Gudi. Devalayam ... they all mean 'temple', and the temples of India are not just places of worship, but are also marvels of awe-inspiring architecture, sculpture and painting.

The colossal Brihadeeswarar Temple in Thanjavur is a UNESCO World Heritage Site.

## CHOLA CLASSICS

Between the 10th and 12th century CE, the Chola kings built spectacular temples in Tamil Nadu. The most famous of these is the **Brihadeeswarar (Shiva) Temple** in Thanjavur, with its exquisite carvings and inscriptions that recorded everything from the deity's jewellery to what the cooks and cleaners were paid! The vimanan (tower) above the shrine is topped by a huge granite slab weighing over 80 tonnes. No one knows how it was lifted up there, as there were no machines then.

The stone Nandi (sacred bull) at the temple is one of the largest in the country. It was crafted outside the temple from a single stone, but the sculptors then found that the gateway was too small to bring it into the temple courtyard. Breaking the gateway would have been considered inauspicious. When everyone was wondering what to do, Saint Karur Siddhar came to the rescue. He smeared the Nandi with a special paste of herbs and oils and it just about managed to slide in through the temple gateway.

WHAT A MOVING STORY!

## DAZZLING DILWARA

The **Dilwara** temples near Mount Abu in Rajasthan, built between the 11th and 13th centuries, are an important pilgrimage centre for Jains. They are built of marble, and celebrated for their finely carved pillars, arches, ceilings and doorways, which come alive with scenes from mythology, and sculptures of animals and dancers.

Do you know how the artisans were persuaded to make many of these intricate carvings? The story goes that they were offered gold equal in weight to the marble dust their work produced! So they grabbed their chisels and went chip, chip, chip.

AAAACHHOO!

GREAT! THERE GOES OUR GOLD!

# for Temples

## ALL ARE WELCOME

**The Golden Temple** or **Harmandir Sahib** in Amritsar, Punjab, is the holiest shrine of the Sikhs. So what's the secret behind its name? Take a look at its covering of glittering gold foil and you'll surely be able to guess! The temple is set in a lake called Amrit Sarovar (Pool of Nectar), and it was built by Guru Arjan Dev, in the 16th century.

The reading of the Sikh holy book, the *Guru Granth Sahib*, goes on 24 hours a day and so does the feeding of pilgrims. Any time is mealtime. Hundreds of volunteers help in preparing the food, as a way of serving God. Anyone who visits the temple is welcome to eat there for free, and more than 70,000 people are fed every day. So if your stomach is going rumble, grumble, growl after all that praying, step into the langar (kitchen/dining area), where beggars and billionaires sit and eat together.

*The Golden Temple is set in the Amrit Sarovar, from which the city of Amritsar gets its name.*

## THAT'S AMAZING!

• The **Venkateswara Temple** in Tirupathi draws more visitors annually than any other temple in India.

• Devotees of all castes and religions throng the **Sai Baba Temple** in Shirdi. The saint preached the message that all living beings, even animals, belong to one family.

• The **Mahabodhi Temple** in Bodh Gaya, Bihar, is one of the oldest brick structures in India. It has been built at the place where Prince Siddhartha attained enlightenment and became the Buddha.

• The **Akshardham Temple** in Delhi is one of the biggest temple complexes in India. It is also a place of education and entertainment and has shrines, shops, parks, musical fountains, robots, and screens showing movies on the life of the founder of the Swamynarayan sect, Bhagwan Swaminarayan.

• Pilgrims to the **Ayyappan Temple** at Sabarimala, Kerala, have to walk through forests, earlier inhabited by wild animals. It is said that devotees who followed a strict code of discipline that purified their mind and heart were never attacked by any beasts.

## for Toys

**The most popular toys today are the battery-operated ones that go whirr, vroom, clickety-clack and, often flash multicoloured lights. Ever wondered what kids played with, way back in time, before there were batteries, plastic or toy factories?**

HOW MANY TIMES SHOULD I TELL YOU? THESE DON'T NEED BATTERIES!

## TOY TALE

The earliest toys that have been discovered in India are whistles, carts and animals made of sticks and clay. They date back to the Indus Valley Civilization, some 5000 years ago.

Down the ages, people began to make toys by recycling whatever materials were available, like leftover bits of wood, bamboo and cloth, metal scraps, clay, discarded cartons, newspapers, and other odds and ends. The chirruping birds, leaping monkeys, slithering snakes, men and women, rattles, drums, flutes and whistles they crafted were inexpensive, fun and eco-friendly too! Such toys were usually sold at village melas or fairs. Nowadays, these have very few takers especially in cities, as children generally prefer factory-made toys.

## TOY TOWNS

**Kondapalli** in Andhra Pradesh is famous for its huge variety of painted wooden toys. You can choose your favourite deity or the ten incarnations of Vishnu, or jolly little animals in bright, shiny colours, or people doing everyday things—women cooking, men milking cows, kids minding cattle, and so on.

If you're looking for wax or clay models of fruits and vegetables, head for Agra, Varanasi, Lucknow or Pune. Want to add to your collection of horses? You'll get these and more, all crafted beautifully from clay, in Bengal. Horses, camels and stuffed cloth toys dressed in exquisite clothes are a speciality of Rajasthan, while South India is known for its wooden playthings and kitchen sets. In fact, the wooden toys of **Channapatna** in Karnataka are so popular that the town is called 'Gombegala Ooru' or the Town of Toys.

*Colourful Channapatna toys*

### for Toys

## PUPPET PARADE

Sure, puppets are toys, but they are also a cool tool for telling stories and educating people. They too have been around for thousands of years and are mentioned in our ancient epics. Puppet shows have always been a part of the fairs and festivals of India. They narrate fascinating tales from the Puranas and epics, of gods and demons and of good triumphing over evil. People believed that this would shoo away evil spirits and disasters, and bring good fortune to all. Some kings also encouraged puppet shows and, in return, puppeteers began to portray the heroic deeds of royalty. Now, the government too uses puppets to spread messages about health and hygiene.

*Traditional kathputli or string puppets*

## PICK A PUPPET

Traditional Indian puppets are of four different types. They are: glove, rod, string and shadow puppets.

• The **glove puppets** have a head, arms and are clad in a long, colourful tunic, which is worn like a glove.

• The **rod puppets** are moved through rods hidden by their costumes.

• The **shadow puppets** are made of leather. These are manipulated behind a white cloth screen with a light shining on them from the back. So the audience does not see the puppets directly but only their shadows on the screen.

• The most popular of all are the **string puppets** or **kathputli** with jointed bodies. The puppeteer handles the puppets through strings tied to various parts of their bodies. They come in different sizes, and the largest, which are about eight feet tall, are used in street plays.

• Most puppeteers are experts in the folk dances and music of their region and perform along with their puppets. The **Yakshagana** of Karnataka, for instance, is a kind of folk play full of music and dance. The Yakshagana puppeteers use the same songs and dance steps, costumes and jewellery for their puppets as they do for themselves!

*A Yakshagana puppeteer in costume*

## for Trees

**Our legends speak of the wish-fulfilling Kalpavriksha Tree in heaven. Although there are no such trees in our country, India does have everything from the banyan, oak, teak and deodar, to weird-sounding ones like the cannon ball tree, the Indian devil tree and the toothbrush tree!**

## TREE TIME

Trees are considered sacred in India, and many of the deities are said to have their personal favourites. For instance, the **bilva** tree is Shiva's chosen one, and the **parijata** is Indra's favourite. The **sandalwood** tree is dear to all the gods. The bark, leaves and roots of many trees are used for making medicines. Also, ancient sages lived in forests and taught their disciples beneath big, shady trees.

HOLLYWOOD, BOLLYWOOD, KOLLYWOOD, SANDALWOOD... IT'S ALL SO CONFUSING!

## WALKING WONDER

India's national tree, the **banyan**, belongs to the fig family. Its branches send down plait-like aerial roots, which turn into thick trunks. This way, a single tree can keep 'walking' and form a huge grove! No wonder, it is popularly called 'bahupada', which means one with many feet in Sanskrit. The banyan is found all over India, and the banias (merchants) would often meet under it and get down to business. When the British who were ruling the country noticed this, they began to call it the 'banyan' tree from the word 'bania'.

Alexander the Great is believed to have camped under a huge banyan tree, which was able to shelter his army of 7000 men. One of the biggest banyans in India, which is at least 250 years old, is in Kolkata. Its main trunk is 13 feet wide, and it has around 3300 smaller trunks and aerial roots, many of which were lost when Cyclone Amphan passed through West Bengal in May 2020.

*Prince Siddhartha achieved enlightenment and became the Buddha after meditating under a peepal tree.*

## TREE OF ENLIGHTENMENT

The **peepal** tree also belongs to the fig family and, like the banyan, is considered sacred by Hindus. The most famous peepal tree is the one in Bodh Gaya, under which Prince Siddhartha meditated and became the Buddha, or the Enlightened One.

## **T** for Trees

## NEEM AND NECTAR

The story goes that when Indra, king of the gods, was carrying a pot of nectar, some of it spilt on the **neem** trees down below on earth. That's how the neem acquired many medicinal properties. In fact it is often called the village pharmacy. Medicines, cosmetics, fertilizers and pesticides are made from different parts of the neem tree. Mahatma Gandhi, for instance, regularly ate neem leaf chutney, because he believed it kept him fit and healthy.

## COCONUT CONFUSION

In South India, coconuts are used in cooking and for rituals. There is an interesting legend about the origin of the **coconut** tree. Once upon a time, a king called Trishanku wanted to go to heaven while keeping his body. He was a good and pious man, so Sage Vishwamitra promised to help him. Through the power of the sage's prayers, Trishanku rose to heaven. But Indra refused to let him in. 'Off with your body, or off you go!' he said, giving Trishanku such a hard poke that he went tumbling down.

Now Vishwamitra, who had made the travel plans for Trishanku, was mighty miffed. 'Stop!' he commanded, and Trishanku found himself dangling between heaven and earth. Vishwamitra propped him up with a long pole, which turned into a coconut tree, with Trishanku's head as the fruit!

## SACRED AND SAFE

Did you think the idea of conserving forests is something new? Actually, long before there were environment protection groups telling people to 'save trees, save the planet', our ancestors were already doing it. There are **sacred groves** across the country, where plants and trees have been protected and worshipped for centuries. No tree can be cut there and no animal or bird is hunted. The best known of these are the devara kadu in Coorg, swami shola in Yelagiri, the kavus of Kerala and the sacred groves in the Khasia and Jaintia Hills of Meghalaya, and in the Aravalli Hills in Rajasthan.

The tall, slender coconut tree can grow to a height of 25 m (about 80 feet).

THANK GOODNESS ISAAC NEWTON WASN'T SITTING UNDER ONE OF THESE!

# for Unani Medicine

*Hakim Ibn Sina's 14-volume work,* The Canon of Medicine, *was the standard medical textbook till the 18th century.*

## GOING PLACES FROM GREECE

Unani medicine, as the name suggests, originated in Greece (which is called **Unan** in Arabic). It was **Hippocrates**, the famous Greek physician, who elevated medicine from being mere mumbo jumbo to a systematic science. So, the theoretical framework of unani medicine is based on the teachings of Hippocrates. After Hippocrates, several Greek, Roman, Arabic and Persian scholars enriched the system and it travelled to many parts of the world under different names like Greco-Arab medicine, Ionian medicine, Arab or Islamic medicine, Oriental medicine and so on.

The fundamental principle of the unani system is that disease is a natural process and the symptoms of a disease are the way the body reacts to it. Unani medicine cures based on the concept of the four **humours** (the four main fluids in the body—phlegm, blood, yellow bile and black bile) whose balance determines our well being.

## INDIA AHOY

Unani medicine as a healing system was primarily described by the Muslim scholar **Hakim Ibn Sina** (also known as Avicenna) in his medical encyclopedia, *The Canon of Medicine*, in 1025 CE. While he was influenced by Greek and Islamic medicine, he also relied on the Indian medical teachings of scholars like **Sushruta** (the father of surgery) and **Charaka** (the father of medicine).

Unani medication first arrived in India around the 12th century with the establishment of the Delhi Sultanate. Ala-ud-din Khilji is believed to have had several unani physicians or hakims in his court.

Even today, unani medicine is among the popular practices in India and there are 40 undergraduate and postgraduate colleges where it is being taught. However, most of the books in the syllabus are written in Arabic, Persian and Urdu, which means an aspirant of unani medicine needs to become a linguist before he trains to be a doctor!

JUST CHECKING YOUR SENSE OF HUMOUR, YOUR HIGHNESS!

# for Union Territories

For administrative purposes and in order to govern the country more efficiently, India has been presently divided into 28 states and eight special regions, which are known as union territories.

## WHAT IS A UNION TERRITORY?

A union territory is an administrative region in India, which is ruled directly by the central government unlike the states of India, which have their own elected governments. The President of India appoints an administrator or lieutenant governor for each union territory.

Union territories have been given special rights in our constitution. This has been done for administrative reasons, for better governance and to safeguard the local culture of that region. Union territories can become states in the future for more efficient administrative control.

DIVIDED WE RULE, BUT UNITED WE STAND?

## WHY WERE THEY FORMED?

The States Reorganization Act of 1956 abolished the British system of provinces and princely states, and new states were drawn based on ethnicity and language. These states were the country's most important administrative units. However, there were some regions which could not be joined to these states because of political, strategic or cultural considerations. They were designated as union territories and came under the central administration.

## THE EXCITING EIGHT

Presently, India has eight union territories. They are the **Andaman and Nicobar Islands**, **Dadra and Nagar Haveli and Daman and Diu**, **Jammu and Kashmir**, **Lakshadweep**, **Chandigarh**, **Ladakh**, **Puducherry** and **The Government of National Capital Territory of Delhi**. Delhi, Jammu and Kashmir and Puducherry operate a little differently from the others. They were given partial statehood and have their own elected legislative assemblies and governments.

### ANDAMAN & NICOBAR ISLANDS

• 572 islands make up the Andaman and Nicobar Islands of which only 34 are permanently inhabited.

• The islands are peopled by many indigenous tribes like the **Jarawas**, the **Onges**, the **Sentinalese**, the **Nicobarese** and the **Shompen**.

• The islands were used by the British as a penal colony and several of our freedom fighters were imprisoned in the notorious **Kala Paani** or Cellular Jail.

An aerial view of the Andaman Islands

# U

## for Union Territories

**DELHI**
Turn to Page 27
**JAMMU AND KASHMIR**
Turn to Page 70
**LADAKH**
Turn to Page 75

## CHANDIGARH

• Chandigarh is the only city in India which serves as the capital of two states—Punjab and Haryana.

• Chandigarh was the first planned city in India post-Independence and is known for its architecture and urban design by architects like **Le Corbusier** and **Pierre Jeanneret**. It was reported to be India's cleanest city in 2010.

• **Nek Chand's Rock Garden** in Chandigarh attracts many visitors because of its bizarre human and animal sculptures made from discarded garbage and junk.

## DADRA AND NAGAR HAVELI AND DAMAN AND DIU

• In November 2019, the Government of India introduced a legislation to merge Daman and Diu and Dadra and Nagar Haveli into a single union territory to be known as Dadra and Nagar Haveli and Daman and Diu, effective from 26 January 2020.

• Dadra and Nagar Haveli is known as the Cherrapunji of western India because of how rainy it is, which is also the reason for its rich biodiversity.

• Although the **Warlis** and their paintings are commonly associated with Maharashtra, they consider Dadra and Nagar Haveli to be their original home.

• For over 450 years, Daman and Diu were part of Portuguese India, along with Goa and Dadra and Nagar Haveli. Goa, Daman, and Diu were incorporated into India on 19 December 1961 by military conquest, but Portugal did not recognize this until 1974.

• Many older people in Daman and Diu still speak Portuguese and two dying Portuguese-based languages called **Língua da Casa** or Home Language (in Daman) and **Língua dos Velhos** or Elders' Language (in Diu).

## LAKSHADWEEP

• Lakshadweep is an archipelago of 12 atolls, three reefs and five submerged banks. A total surface area of just 32 sq km makes it India's tiniest union territory.

• The **Amindivi** and **Laccadive** group of islands together with **Minicoy** Island form the coral islands of India. All these islands of Lakshadweep have been formed by layers of corals and have beautiful reefs close to their shores.

## PUDUCHERRY

• Puducherry is the only union territory whose four constituent districts—**Yanam**, **Karaikal**, **Mahe** and **Pondicherry**—are located in different states.

• A former French colony, Puducherry is popularly known as the French Riviera of the East and is famous for spiritual centres like the **Aurobindo Ashram** and **Auroville**.

*An old French-style building in Puducherry*

## for Universities

From the ancient universities of Nalanda and Taxila to the present-day IITs, IIMs and IISc, education and higher learning have always been given great prominence in India.

## THE WORLD'S OLDEST UNIVERSITY?

**Takshashila** or **Taxila** was an early Hindu and Buddhist centre of learning in Rawalpindi district, which was a part of India before the Partition. Some scholars date the university's existence back to the 5th century BCE, which certainly makes it the world's oldest university. But since it did not function under one authority, it has not been able to stake claim to the record.

It is believed that a student entered Takshashila at the age of 16 after completing a basic education. He then had the option of picking from 64 different fields of study like the Vedas, the arts, grammar, philosophy, ayurveda, politics, astronomy, commerce, law and futurology. There were even some curious subjects like the art of discovering hidden treasures and understanding encrypted messages! Some of the famous students graduating from here included **Charaka**, the father of ayurvedic medicine, **Chanakya**, who wrote his well-known treatise *Arthashastra* when he was at Takshashila, and the ancient Sanskrit grammarian **Panini**.

## HOW COOL IS THIS SCHOOL?

Examinations were considered wasteful and students were not required to pass one to complete their studies at Takshashila. The process of teaching, however, was thorough. Unless the student mastered one subject completely to the teacher's satisfaction, he was not allowed to proceed to the next one. No convocations were held and no degrees awarded, since it was believed that knowledge was its own reward. What's more, education was considered too sacred to be paid for, so no fees were charged! Tempted to send your principal to get some useful tips from Takshashila?

How do we know all this? Well, Takshashila is described in great detail in the Jataka tales, written in Sri Lanka, and in the extensive travel writings of the Chinese travellers **Faxian** and **Xuanzang**.

A view of the site where Takshashila University once flourished.

## for Universities

## NALANDA LEADS THE WAY

**Nalanda University** was an ancient centre of higher learning in Bihar, India. Located about 88 km south-east of Patna, it flourished for 600 years from the 5th to the 12th centuries under the reign of the Gupta kings, mainly Emperor Shakraditya, and supported by the patronage of Buddhist rulers like Harsha.

Nalanda has many firsts to its credit. It was the world's first residential university and had dormitories for students and teachers. At its peak, it accommodated over 10,000 students and 2000 teachers! The university was considered an architectural masterpiece with its high walls and an elegant entrance gate. There were eight separate compounds inside, ten temples and many classrooms and meditation halls. Several lakes and parks dotted the campus. The library, which was the largest in the ancient world, housed many sacred manuscripts. The subjects taught at Nalanda covered almost every field of learning. The university attracted students and scholars from countries like Korea, Japan, China, Tibet, Indonesia, Persia and Turkey.

*Ruins at the Nalanda University site*

## A LIBRARY TO DIE FOR!

The library of Nalanda University was a magnificent complex and had thousands of manuscripts on religion, grammar, logic, literature, astrology, astronomy and medicine. Called the **Dharmaganja**, the mighty complex 'soared above the mists in the sky' according to a description by Xuanzang. It had three large buildings: the **Ratnasagara**, the **Ratnadadhi**, and the **Ratnaranjaka**. The Ratnadadhi or the Ocean of Gems was nine storeys tall and stored the most sacred manuscripts. The library was so advanced that it even had a classification scheme developed by Panini!

Nalanda was ransacked and destroyed by an army under Bakhtiyar Khilji in 1193 CE. The library, which was so vast, is supposed to have burned for three months after the invaders set fire to it! In 2010, the Indian Parliament passed a bill approving plans to restore this ancient centre of learning as the modern Nalanda International University dedicated to postgraduate research.

## MODERN MARVELS

With such a glorious tradition to draw from, it is no wonder that modern India can boast of some educational powerhouses like the **Indian Institute of Technology** (IIT), the **Indian Institute of Management** (IIM) and the **Indian Institute of Science** (IISc).

• The first IIT and IIM were both set up in West Bengal, in Kharagpur and Kolkata, in the years 1950 and 1961, respectively.

• An accidental meeting took place between Jamsetji Tata and Swami Vivekananda on a ship in 1893. They discussed Tata's grand plan of bringing the steel industry to India. This conversation was the main reason behind the setting up of the IISc in Bangalore in 1909.

## for Varanasi

The city of temples, the holy city of India, the religious capital of India, the city of lights, the city of learning . . . no other place in India encompasses all these descriptions better than Varanasi!

## SPIRITUAL HOTSPOT

Varanasi, also called **Banaras** or **Kashi**, is a sacred city on the banks of River Ganga in Uttar Pradesh. It is believed to be the holiest of the Saptapuri or seven sacred cities in Hinduism. Hindus come to Varanasi to wash away their sins and attain moksha or salvation of the soul from the cycle of rebirth. This is because Varanasi is considered a 'crossing place', where mortals can pass over to the other world. And oh, the crossing works both ways, because gods and goddesses too can come down to earth to bathe in the Ganga! Varanasi is one of the oldest continuously inhabited cities in the world.

## A CITY OF LEARNING AND BURNING

Named after the confluence of two rivers, Varuna and Asi, the city has grown around the ghats (steps) along the riverfront. Each ghat is in the shape of a linga and honours Lord Shiva. Most of the ghats are for bathing, while some like the **Manikarnika Ghat** and the **Harishchandra Ghat** are used as cremation sites. The story goes that Shiva and Parvati were having a bath in the Ganga when their precious ornaments—mani (jewel) and karnika (earrings)—were swept away by the swift river currents. In anger, Shiva cursed that the place would be used only to burn the dead.

**Dashashwamedh Ghat** is probably the oldest and most spectacular of the ghats. According to one legend, Lord Brahma created it to welcome Lord Shiva to Varanasi. Take a trip down the river today and you can see devotees bathing, meditating and performing rituals here every morning to greet the sun. And, at sunset, priests perform the spectacular Ganga aarti, with incense, lamps and candles, to offer prayers to the river.

Varanasi has attracted pilgrims from time immemorial. The Buddha is believed to have visited here in 500 BCE after he achieved enlightenment. He then travelled to Sarnath nearby, to share his teachings with the people who lived there.

*The ghats by River Ganga in Varanasi*

## for Varanasi

## A BITE TO EAT?

Since Varanasi is so holy to the Hindus, people cremate bodies here and scatter the ashes in the Ganga. However, there are many who cannot afford the wood needed to burn the entire body. They end up disposing dead bodies that are not fully burnt in the river. To get rid of the floating body parts, some 25,000 special omnivorous turtles have been bred and released into the river as part of India's massive **Ganga Action Plan**, to clean up one of the world's most polluted river systems. These turtles can consume dead human flesh and it takes ten adult turtles about three days to consume an entire human body. The turtles have been so cleverly trained that they only go after dead meat without bothering devotees who bathe and swim in the river!

*The Banaras Hindu University campus*

## WOW, VARANASI!

• The **Kashi Vishwanath Temple** in Varanasi is one of the most holy Hindu temples dedicated to Lord Shiva. In fact, there are about 23,000 temples to see here, which is why it is said that if Delhi is the capital of the politicians, Varanasi is the capital of the gods!

• The **Banaras Hindu University** at Varanasi is one of the largest residential universities of Asia.

• Tulsidas composed his epic poem *Shri Ramcharitmanas* at Varanasi.

• No trip to Varanasi is complete without chewing the famous **Banarasi paan** (betel leaf). The paan, though, is not from Banaras at all! The leaf, which is called maghai, is grown in Bihar.

*The popular and delicious Banarasi paan*

# for Villages

'The soul of India is in its villages,' said the Father of the Nation, Mahatma Gandhi. And rightly so, for 68 per cent of India lives in one of its 6,40,867 villages to this day!

## LORE AND BEHOLD

It is interesting to see that the concept of villages was not clearly defined in ancient India during the Indus Valley Civilization. Archaeologists have found the remains of several well-planned cities and towns, including Harappa and Mohenjodaro.

The history of Indian villages mainly begins in the Vedic period, when kingdoms were made up of one major city and several villages. Generally, a cluster of houses formed a village and the surrounding land was cultivated by the villagers. The concept of villages flourished under Chandragupta Maurya, who ruled in 323 BCE, and they gradually became an important part of the Indian social system.

## FARMING OUT JOBS

Do you know which occupation provides employment to the most number of Indians and is the backbone of our economy? Information technology? Engineering? Well, you'll be surprised that **agriculture** in the villages provides employment to more Indians (over 50 per cent) than any other economic sector! With such a strong agricultural base, India is the largest producer of fresh fruit, pulses, ginger, black pepper and milk in the world.

*A typical Indian village*

## ISN'T THAT WHACKY?

• Most Indians have complete faith in God, but the people of **Shani Shingnapur** village in Maharashtra have taken their belief to new levels. Since Shanidev appeared in the dreams of one of the villagers many decades ago and declared that there was no need to build any closed temple for him and that he preferred being worshipped under the open skies, the villagers have never built doors at the entrance of their houses. Houses only have windows and curtained doorways to this day!

• For creativity at its best, make a trip to **Bhadrapura** village in Karnataka, where villagers are named after every amenity that the village lacks! So there's a 'High Court', 'Gramophone', 'Bus', 'Train', 'Military' and even a 'Dollar'!

• Sure, humans and animals can coexist peacefully, but how about a village where people get along famously with cobras? Welcome to **Shetpal** village in the state of Maharashtra. The houses here are built with rafters so cobras can slip in and out of them easily! What's more, no one in the village has been bitten by a cobra to date!

# for Wagah

A village that was divided when India and Pakistan were partitioned in 1947, Wagah is the site of an elaborate Lowering of Flags ceremony that is viewed by thousands of people on either side of the border every day!

## A THIN DIVIDING LINE

Wagah is the only road border crossing between Pakistan and India and lies on the historic Grand Trunk Road between the cities of Amritsar in India and Lahore in Pakistan. It is the village through which the Radcliffe Line, the boundary line that divided India and Pakistan during Partition, was drawn on 17 August 1947. The eastern half of the village came to India while the western half went to Pakistan. The Wagah border is at a distance of 27 km from Amritsar and 29 km from Lahore.

## CEREMONY OF CHEER AND CONTEMPT

**The Lowering of Flags** or **Beating the Retreat** ceremony is a daily military practice that the security forces of India (Border Security Force) and Pakistan (Pakistan Rangers) have jointly followed at the Wagah border since 1959. The show, which begins at sundown, lasts for about 45 minutes and is watched by hundreds of cheering spectators on both sides.

The drill includes soldiers marching with long, brisk strides, high kicks, foot stamping and smart salutes as each side tries to outdo the other in the sound of their footsteps, the pace of their marching and even in the exchange of angry looks! As the sun sets, the heavy iron gates are opened and the flags of the two countries are lowered simultaneously. The flags are then folded and carried back to their respective countries, after which the gates are slammed shut. The ceremony has often been described as a unique display of 'carefully choreographed contempt'.

A Pakistani soldier and an Indian soldier try to outdo each other at Wagah.

## WAH, WAGAH!

• Wagah was the only road link between the two countries before the opening of the **Aman Setu** in Kashmir in 1999.

• Guards who participate in the drill are carefully selected on the basis of their imposing height, stature, and even the size of their moustaches! Since July 2011, women guards of the BSF have also started taking part in the ceremony.

• The **Delhi-Lahore bus** is a passenger bus service connecting Delhi with Lahore via the border at Wagah. It is symbolic of Indo-Pak efforts to maintain peaceful relations.

## for Wazwan

What do most Indians do when we meet for family get-togethers or to celebrate festivals and weddings? Eat, of course, and meals with multiple courses at that!

## WONDERFUL WAZWAN

Ever heard the popular reference to Kashmir being heaven on earth? Well, the breathtaking beauty of the place notwithstanding, one of the reasons for the description could be the delectable wazwan! It is a traditional 36-course Kashmiri Muslim meal, cooked mainly at weddings and festivals. The preparations are traditionally done by a **vasta waza** or head chef, who is assisted by a court of wazas or chefs. Most of the dishes in a wazwan are meat-based (lamb or chicken).

Guests are seated in groups of four and share the meal out of a large metal plate called the tarami. Traditionally, the meal begins by invoking the name of Allah and a ritual washing of hands in a basin called the tash-t-nari. Then, the taramis are brought in, heaped with rice and flavourful meats. The meal ends with a sweet treat, the yummy phirni. But wait, it isn't fully done till you wash the meal down with a cup of hot kahwah, the local green tea laced with saffron strands and crushed almonds. Burp!

And what do you do if you aren't a hearty eater? Don't worry, there is a delightful solution at hand. To enjoy the flavours of every course of the wazwan, guests are given bags in which they can pack the extra food and take it home!

The delicious Onam sadya is a feast fit for kings.

## EAT, PRAY, LOVE

Want to eat to your heart's content in Tamil Nadu? Then, dig into a **virundhu saapaadu**! Virundhu means feast and saapaadu a full course meal, and in combination, that's a feast fit for a king! Served on a banana leaf, there's a specific place for each of the dishes that make up the meal and a particular order in which they have to be served. Once the food is served, all you need to do is to dig right in with your fingers!

And if you happen to go to nearby Kerala, make sure it is during Onam, so you can treat your stomach to the delicious, nine-course, strictly vegetarian **Onam sadya**. Prepared in honour of King Mahabali whose spirit is said to visit Kerala at this time, people whip up a grand feast in order to convey to the king that they still enjoy the prosperity he had ushered in during his rule. The good thing is that the king is there only in spirit, but you're there for real, so greet, eat and enjoy the treat!

The **langar** or community meal is a unique food tradition of the Sikhs. Langar could also mean the community kitchen in a gurdwara. A langar meal is simple and vegetarian, and it is served to anyone who is hungry, irrespective of religion, 365 days of the year. What's more, it's free!

IF PEOPLE GET DOGGY BAGS, WHAT WILL WE GET? PEOPLE BAGS?

## for Wedding

Swishing silks, fragrant flowers, glittering gold, hennaed hands, religious rituals, bedecked bride and bridegroom, garrulous guests . . . there's nothing more showy and celebratory than the great Indian wedding!

The bride and the bridegroom performing traditional Hindu wedding rituals.

## CUSTOM-MADE IN HEAVEN

If there's any celebration that showcases India as a melting pot of religions, cultures and customs, it has got be the big fat Indian wedding! From ancient times, Indian marriages have been packed with customs, rituals and traditions, irrespective of whether they are Hindu, Muslim or Christian ceremonies. So, if a Hindu couple has to go through the **saptapadi** or seven steps around the sacred fire to tie the knot, a Muslim couple has to sign a formal contract for their **nikaah** or marriage ceremony to take place and the Christians have to say their vows and be blessed by a priest to be joined in holy matrimony. While arranged marriage is the preferred Indian choice, where parents choose a life partner for their children, there are no hard and fast rules about the right way to get married in India . . . as long as you do!

## GOOD GOD!

Lord Krishna is believed to have had eight main wives and 16,000 minor wives. He is even supposed to have eloped with his principal wife and queen, Rukmini, upon her request! King Dasharatha, Rama's father, had three wives, and Draupadi, by a quirk of fate, ended up marrying the five Pandava princes.

If you thought only men had their way when it came to marriage, our legends are full of stories of queens who chose their own life partners through **swayamvaras**, where they could pick the best man from among a gathering of eligible suitors. Sita, Draupadi and Damayanti all chose their own husbands. They even made the prospective suitors work hard and pass tests in order to win their hand in marriage!

Fortunately, the law of the land today permits all Indians (excluding Muslims) to have only one spouse.

# for Wedding

## IT'S ALL IN THE STARS

Since marriage is all about finding the right spouse, we Indians can thank our lucky stars that we have the stars for help! The matching of the **janam kundali** or astrological chart plotted at the time of birth with that of a potential life partner's is a common practice. The maximum points for any match can be 36 and the minimum points 18. So, if you score under 18 in the test, don't worry, simply blame the stars!

## MARRY IN A HURRY

If you want to keep things short, simple and sweet, you could opt for an **Arya Samaj** wedding. A unique Vedic tradition, it was conceived by Dayanand Saraswati in 1875 to reduce the ritualistic nature of weddings and cut down on the excessive money and time spent on them. Simplicity is the key of this wedding and ceremonies are completed in under an hour. Rites and rituals are not performed to any specific deity. The couple chants the mantras and says the marriage vows, which are explained to them in a language they understand.

## SHAA . . . HA . . . HA . . . DI!

• Sarsaul, a small town in Uttar Pradesh, has redefined the meaning of the words wedding hospitality. Guests from the bridegroom's side are not greeted with a sprinkling of flowers and rose water. Instead, tomatoes and potatoes are hurled at them, followed by a round of choice abuse. Well, this is done in the belief that a relationship which begins on a sour note at first is likely to turn sweet and loving later!

• At a Tamil Iyer wedding, just as the groom is about to step on to the dais for the wedding ceremony, he has an apparent change of mind and decides to head to Kashi to become a sanyasi! So off he goes with a pair of simple sandals on his feet and umbrella, palm leaf fan and Bhagavad Gita in hand. But that's only until the bride's father or brother runs after him and sweet-talks him into coming back, which he is usually more than willing to do!

*Raja Ravi Varma's* Galaxy of Musicians *woven on the world's most expensive sari*

## SIX YARDS OF OPULENCE

Where could the world's most expensive and grand wedding sari be woven? In India, of course. It was made by the **Chennai Silks**, a popular sari showroom in Chennai. The sari features reproductions of 11 paintings by the celebrated Indian artist Raja Ravi Varma, including his famous 'Galaxy of Musicians'. It took 30 weavers a total of 4760 man-hours to create the jewel-encrusted garment. The cost? A whopping 39,31,627 rupees! And its weight? Nine kilos only!

# for X Avatars of Vishnu

**Hindus believe that whenever the forces of evil take over the world, Lord Vishnu comes to the rescue. To protect the good and destroy the wicked, he descends to earth in various forms called incarnations or avatars. His top ten amazing avatars are called Dashavatar.**

## MATSYA AVATAR

**Saving the Scriptures:** Vishnu's first incarnation was the Matsya (Fish) Avatar. He came as a giant golden fish to recover the Vedas (the holy scriptures of the Hindus), which had been stolen by an asura and were hidden at the bottom of the ocean.

## KURMA AVATAR

**Moving Mountains:** Ages ago, the devas and asuras started churning the cosmic ocean to obtain the nectar of immortality. They used Mount Mandara as the churning rod, but it began to sink. Enter Vishnu in his Kurma (Tortoise) Avatar. Diving into the water, he balanced the mountain on his back till the job was done.

## VARAHA AVATAR

**Boar Lore:** The asura Hiranyaksha once imprisoned Mother Earth at the bottom of the cosmic ocean. Vishnu came thundering down in the form of Varaha the Boar and killed Hiranyaksha after a fierce battle. He then rescued Mother Earth by scooping her up in his great big tusks.

WOW! HOW COOL! THAT REALLY IS SOME HIRAN-ACTION!

## NARASIMHA AVATAR

**Mighty Man-lion:** The wicked asura Hiranyakashipu, who was Hiranyaksha's elder brother, had been granted a boon that he would not be killed by a human, god or animal, inside the house or outside, during daytime or at night. When his atrocities became unbearable, the people prayed to Vishnu, who came down as Narasimha (half-man, half-lion). It was twilight, neither day nor night. And on the palace threshold, neither indoors nor outdoors, Narasimha tore Hiranyakashipu apart with his claws!

WHAT'S WITH ALL THE VIOLENCE?

UMM...

## VAMANA AVATAR

**Slick Trick:** The asura king Mahabali had conquered heaven and earth, and the gods grew jittery. So Vishnu went to him disguised as a learned dwarf (Vamana), and asked for all the land he could cover in three steps. The king readily agreed.

Vishnu, however, grew and grew. In one step, he covered the earth and with his next the heavens. There was nowhere he could take the third step, so the king bent his head and asked him to place his foot on it. Vishnu was pleased Mahabali had kept his promise, so he crowned him king of the underworld.

## PARASHURAMA AVATAR

**Angry Avenger:** Once upon a time, some kings turned into tyrants and began to oppress saints and sages. So Vishnu came down to earth as mighty Parashurama or Rama-with-the-axe, to destroy these rulers and restore order and justice.

# for X Avatars of Vishnu

## BUDDHA AVATAR

**Prince of Peace**: In this incarnation, Vishnu was born a prince. He, however, gave up his throne to spread the message of peace and love. As Buddha, the Enlightened One, he guided others to the right path.

*Prince Siddhartha attained enlightenment under the Bodhi tree in Bodh Gaya, and became the Buddha.*

## KALKI AVATAR

**Far into the Future**: Kalki, the 10th and last avatar of Vishnu is yet to appear. It is believed that he will arrive on a white horse, carry a blazing sword and destroy the wicked. With his arrival, the present age, Kali Yuga, will end, and the Golden Age will begin.

*Parashurama or Rama-with-the-axe*

## RAMA AVATAR

**Inspiring Ideal:** Vishnu was born as Rama, the Prince of Ayodhya, to put an end to the atrocities of Ravana, the asura king of Lanka. When Rama and his wife Sita were living in exile in the forest, Ravana kidnapped Sita. Rama then fought and killed Ravana in battle and rescued Sita.

## KRISHNA AVATAR

**Wise Warrior:** Throughout his life, Krishna fought the wicked. As a baby he sucked the life out of the murderous demoness Pootana. Then he killed various asuras, the tyrant Kamsa, and the monster snake Kaliya. Krishna was as smart as he was strong. The advice given by him to the Pandava hero Arjuna during the Mahabharata war became the holy book, Bhagavad Gita.

WHAT ABOUT *THIS* GUY?

# for Xuanzang

Many travellers have visited India since ancient times—scholars, teachers, pilgrims, traders, missionaries, spies, adventurers, and those who had to travel ... because they were crazy about travel, or just plain crazy!

## XUANZANG: STEADFAST SCHOLAR

In the past, travellers usually went bumpity-bump on horses, mules or camels, braving terrible dangers, for on the way lurked bandits and beasts waiting to pounce. One such traveller was **Xuanzang** or **Hiuen-Tsang** (602–664), a Chinese Buddhist monk. The Emperor of China had then forbidden travel in the lawless western regions of the country. But Xuanzang had a dream. He was determined to go to India to study and learn Buddha's teachings.

Hiding by day and travelling at night, the resolute Xuanzang passed through various kingdoms, facing many hardships along the way. Once, he lost his way in the desert. As he lay dying of hunger and thirst, he prayed with all his heart, and by some miracle, his horse guided him to an oasis. From there, he journeyed across icy mountain ranges and finally reached India.

For 13 years, he wandered through the subcontinent, visiting sacred Buddhist sites and monasteries. He also stayed for a few years at Nalanda University in Bihar, studying and debating with the other scholars there.

I WONDER WHAT MEDIUM HE TOOK HIS CLASSES IN.

## HOME, SWEET HOME!

On his return to China, Xuanzang wrote about his travels. He also translated into Chinese hundreds of sacred Buddhist texts, which he had collected during his journey. In fact, when these books were lost in India, they were translated back from the Chinese copies!

## FAXIAN: WALKING WONDER

Xuanzang had followed in the footsteps of **Faxian** or **Fa Hien** (337–424). He was the first Chinese Buddhist monk who came to India to visit holy sites and collect sacred Buddhist texts. Faxian actually walked all the way from China, across deserts and mountains. He later wrote about his journey, and commented that it had been incredibly dangerous because the dragons that lived among the mountain peaks, whipped up poisonous winds and blinding snowstorms!

*Xuanzang, intrepid traveller, scholar and translator*

for Xuanzang

## TRAVEL TALES

From way back, travellers have written books that fizz with information about India, its people, and their customs. Their descriptive accounts of the splendours of royal courts, the significance of religious ceremonies and the details of the everyday life of common people are a valuable source of evidence that has made the reconstruction of our history easier. The stars were: **Megasthenes** (Greek ambassador), **Sir Thomas Roe** (English ambassador), **Al Beruni** (mathematician and scientist), and countless others such as . . .

## IBN BATTUTA: VALIANT VOYAGER

**Ibn Battuta** (1304–1368) of Morocco was one of the world's greatest travellers. He set out on a pilgrimage to Mecca when he was just 21, and did not return home for the next 24 years! Instead, he travelled across Africa, Europe and Asia, covering over 1,20,000 km.

Ibn Battuta spent nearly nine years in India, and Sultan Muhammad bin Tughlaq even made him a judge. A great honour, indeed, but he was soon in big trouble. He never knew when the eccentric sultan would shower him with gifts and treat him as a trusted favourite, or when he would turn around and roar, 'You miserable traitor! Off with your head!'

Somehow, Ibn Battuta managed to escape the country by persuading Tughlaq to send him to faraway China as his ambassador. When he returned home, he wrote a fantastic book on his travels called—what else!— *Rihlah* (Travels).

## NICCOLAI MANUCCI: TRICK OR TREAT

**Niccolai Manucci** (1653–1708) ran away from his home in Venice at the age of 14 and came to India. Dara Shikoh and his brother Aurangzeb were then fighting for the Mughal throne, and Manucci joined Dara as a gunner. But Dara, whose army had more barbers, butchers, tinkers and tailors than soldiers, was defeated and executed by Aurangzeb.

So Manucci then did a quick job switch. He became a quack, an ambassador and a writer. His famous work, *Storia do Mogor*, which describes Mughal life and history, was written in Italian, French and Portuguese. This multi-tasking trickster also pretended to help people by driving out demons with ear-splitting curses and evil-smelling fumes!

## for Yatra

For thousands of years, Hindus have set forth on yatras (pilgrimages) to holy mountains and cities, bathed in sacred rivers, and joined the jostling crowds at colourful melas celebrating gods, saints and even animal heroes!

## THE FAMOUS FOUR

Many Hindus consider the **char dham yatra** ('char dham' means four holy abodes of the divine) the most important pilgrimage of all. The char dham include **Badrinath** in the north, **Rameswaram** in the south, **Dwarka** in the west and **Puri** in the east. (The northern four—Badrinath, Kedarnath, Gangotri and Yamunotri—are also known as char dham.) So what makes the char dham sacred?

BUT ALWAYS REMEMBER: ALL WALK AND NO PLAY WILL MAKE JACK A TIRED BOY!

The Nizamuddin Dargah in Delhi

## BLESSED BADRINATH

According to legend, Vishnu once sat on a mountain meditating for the welfare of all living beings. He did not stir for hundreds of years. And all that while, his beloved spouse Lakshmi refused to leave his side. As she stood there sheltering Vishnu from the fierce sun, she turned into a sacred Badri (bael) tree! So the place came to be called Badrinath. That's not all. In a cave near Badrinath, Sage Vyasa is said to have written the Mahabharata. And the Pandavas, the heroes of this epic, also passed through Badrinath on their way to heaven.

The Badrinath Temple is dedicated to Lord Vishnu.

Hee Hee

## PILGRIM'S PROGRESS

Yatras are a part of other religions too, although they may be called by different names. For instance, Christians visit the Basilica of Bom Jesus in Goa, where the body of St Francis Xavier rests in a silver casket. The Velankanni Church in Tamil Nadu, built where a vision of the Virgin Mary is said to have been seen, draws huge crowds as well.

The country is dotted with several holy Muslim sites, many of which attract Muslims and Hindus alike, like the dargah of the Sufi saint Nizamuddin Auliya in Delhi, and that of Khwaja Moinuddin Chisti in Ajmer.

# for Yatra

## REVERED RAMESWARAM

When Lord Rama was living in exile in the forest, his wife Sita was kidnapped by Ravana, king of Lanka. In order to rescue her, Rama travelled to Rameswaram, the southernmost tip of the Indian peninsula. From there he is said to have built a bridge across the sea to Lanka. This came to be known as Ramasethu. It is from Rameswaram that Rama embarked on his rescue mission to Lanka, where he defeated and killed Ravana and freed Sita.

BROTHER RAMA, DO WE REALLY NEED TO BUILD THIS BRIDGE? CAN'T WE JUST TAKE A FLIGHT?

## DAZZLING DWARAKA

Dwaraka is sacred because Lord Krishna is said to have dwelt in this splendid city of gem-studded palaces, gardens and lakes. Some years after the Mahabharata War, after Lord Krishna died, his clansmen the Yadavas began fighting bitterly among themselves. The story goes that Arjuna went to Dwaraka to bring Krishna's grandsons and the Yadava ladies to safety. After Arjuna left, the oceans rose and submerged the city. Present-day Dwaraka was built there much later.

A chariot being readied for the Puri Rath Yatra

## PURI'S PUZZLE

Mention Puri—not the one on your plate swimming in aam ras, but in Orissa—and everyone thinks of its annual rath yatra. That's when the deities, Jagannath (Lord Krishna), Balabhadra (Krishna's brother) and Subhadra (Krishna's sister), are taken out in giant chariots from Puri's most visited temple in a spectacular procession. So what's the story behind these deities?

Once upon a time, King Indradyumna found a glowing log floating in the sea. He built a beautiful temple and then looked for a carpenter to carve the three deities from the wood. Vishwakarma came to the king in disguise and offered to do the carving. He had one condition: no one was to enter the temple until the work was done.

Days passed, but the temple door remained shut, and there was not a sound from within. So they forced the door open . . . and the carpenter vanished leaving the deities unfinished. But a voice told King Indradyumna to install them anyway, and so he obeyed.

## for Yoga

**Yoga is over 5000 years old, yet it is a hot favourite with people today. It comes from India, but has now spread all over the world. Millions practise it, for they believe it keeps them fit and relaxed.**

*Yogasanas help to keep both body and mind healthy.*

## WHAT IS YOGA?

If you imagine yoga is about tying yourself into knots or lying on a bed of nails, think again. Yoga is like a branch in the tree of Hinduism, and it has a much higher spiritual goal—enlightenment. There are many forms of yoga and they help to keep the body, mind and spirit healthy and balanced. In fact, various medical problems, such as blood pressure, diabetes, etc. can be controlled through certain forms of yoga like pranayama (breath control) and asanas or postures—sitting, standing, balancing, bending or twisting.

## THE SAGE AND THE STUDENT

Seals discovered in the Indus Valley sites, dating back 5000 years, show deities in yogic poses. However, it was **Sage Patanjali** who put together a system of yoga 2200 years ago.

According to legend, Sage Patanjali was an incarnation of the divine serpent, Adisesha. He was sent down to earth by Lord Vishnu to help people by teaching yoga. Many begged to be his students. Patanjali agreed but on two conditions. 'You must be punctual,' he said. 'And while I teach there must always be a screen between me and everyone else.'

The students nodded and the lessons began. One day, however, a curious student moved the screen. As Sage Patanjali had been teaching them in the form of the serpent Adisesha, his fiery breath burnt the boys to ashes. There was, however, one latecomer who was saved. The sage refused to teach him, but relented after his student pleaded with him. What he taught the boy has come down to us as the *Yoga Sutras* of Patanjali, and these teachings form the basis of yoga.

# for Zero

The zero comes from India, and so does the related system of numbers used by most people today—that is 1, 2, 3, and so on. These numbers are called Hindu–Arabic numerals, because they spread from India to the Middle East and Europe through Arab traders.

## ZERO, THE HERO

The Sanskrit word for zero is 'shunya', which means empty. The Arabs translated it as 'sifr', from which we get the English words cypher and zero. Don't be fooled by this, for the zero has some fantastic uses. Everything anyone does on a computer—whether it's playing video games or getting a plane to drop a bomb on the enemy—needs instructions in what is called the binary code. This code is made up of just two numbers, 1 and 0, arranged in various sets of combinations.

IF *ZERO* IS SO VALUABLE, HOW COME MY PARENTS ARE SO ANNOYED WHEN I GET IT IN MY MATHS TESTS?

The Zero Milestone at Nagpur

## DID YOU KNOW?

• One of the earliest written records of zero in India is a stone inscription from 876 CE. It mentions a garden in **Gwalior**, whose dimensions are 187 by 270 hastas (1 hasta = 45 cm). Enough flowers were grown there to make 50 garlands a day for the local temple. The numbers 270 and 50 look very similar to the way they are today.

• The British who once ruled India considered **Nagpur** the centre of the country. They put up the **Zero Milestone** there, with a pillar and four horses for the four directions. The names of the major cities and their distances from the Zero Milestone are carved on the pillar.

• In **Sikkim**, near the Chinese border, is a place called **Zero Point**. Absolutely no one is allowed to go beyond this except the Indian Army.

• Roman numerals were earlier used in the West, and this system had no zero. Can you imagine what it would be like? For instance, if your favourite cricketer scored 80 runs, the score card would read LXXX, and if he scored 88, it would be even longer: LXXXVIII!

# for Zoos

Want to wave to a wombat without going to Australia? Or say 'Hello!' to a hippo without trudging through the African jungles? Just head for one of our zoological gardens where you will find wild animals from all over the world.

## WHY HAVE ZOOS?

Human beings have hunted animals and destroyed many jungles, which has resulted in several species losing their habitats (their natural homes). They are now endangered and could die out altogether. Modern zoos like the **Chennai Zoo** (**Arignar Anna Zoological Park**) and the **Delhi Zoo** help them survive by providing proper food and large natural surroundings. They also have conservation programmes to make sure the animals stay safe and increase in number.

Arignar Anna Zoological Park

WHY DID WE COME *HERE?* THERE ARE NO DINOSAURS TO SEE!

## DID YOU KNOW?

• The **Alipore Zoo (Kolkata Zoological Gardens)** in West Bengal, is one of the largest and earliest zoos in the country. It was established in 1876, on a tiny budget of Rs 5000 and a few animals donated by a German named Carl Schwendler, who was promptly dubbed father of the zoo! The first handbook on the captive care of wild animals in India was written by Ram Brahma Sanyal, superintendent of the Alipore Zoo, in 1892. The zoo now has several rare animals including the white tiger, royal Bengal tiger, and the great Indian one-horned rhinoceros. Migratory birds like the sarus crane come there in winter.

• One of the most popular zoos in South India, the **Mysore Zoo (**also called the **Sri Chamarajendra Zoological Garden)**, was opened in 1892. It has more elephants than any other zoo in India. Most exciting of all, anyone can adopt the animals there because it has an adopt-an-animal programme. So does the **Nandankanan Zoological Park** in Orissa, which is noted for its white tigers. It also has a breeding programme for the gharial, black panther and pangolin. Can you guess what is special about the **Sri Venkateshwara Zoological Park** in Tirupati? All the animals there have been mentioned in our ancient writings such as the Ramayana, Mahabharata and Panchatantra! The message is that our ancestors thought animals and birds had an important role to play and we should protect them too.

Photo Credits